Home in Your Pack

Home in Your Pack

The Modern Handbook of Backpacking

BRADFORD ANGIER

Collier Books, New York, New York

Collier-Macmillan Limited, London

The Macmillan Company
866 Third Avenue, New York, N.Y. 10022
Collier-Macmillan Canada Ltd., Toronto, Ontario

Home in Your Pack was originally published
in a hardcover edition by Stackpole Books
and is reprinted by arrangement.

Library of Congress Catalog Card
Number: 70-187069

FIRST COLLIER BOOKS EDITION 1972

Printed in the United States of America

Contents

1/ Walking Away from It All

1

Where in the Land to Go

Throughout this country, you can find vast stretches of unspoiled and practically uninhabited wilderness. Here you can take your pack. You can fish and photograph and live with nature for almost as long as you will, and have a glorious and totally different adventure you'll never forget.

All this can be done at hardly any expense. The most costly factor, as a matter of fact, will be your time. Once you have assembled your small outfit and have reached your jumping-off place, you can journey and sight-see at no further outlay than for the food you'd eat anyway, for less than it would cost you to live at home.

Furthermore you are entirely footloose and independent, free to roam and sleep where you will. You need rely on no one, and there is none of the care and cost of boats, cycles, automobiles, and pack animals.

"Hiking a ridge, a meadow, a river bottom, is as healthy a form of exercise as one can get," says Supreme Court Justice William O. Douglas:

Hiking seems to put all the body calls back into rhythm. Ten to twenty miles on a trail puts one to bed with his cares unraveled. Hiking—and climbing, too—are man's most natural exercises. They introduce him again to the wonders of nature and teach him the beauty of the woods and fields in winter as well as in spring. They also teach him how to take care of himself and his neighbors in times of adversity.

We need exercise as individuals. We need to keep physically fit and alert as people. . . . "History is the sound of heavy boots going upstairs and the rustle of satin slippers coming down." Nations that are soft and sleek—people who get all their exercise and athletics vicariously—will not survive when the competition is severe and adversity is at hand. It is imperative that America stay fit. For today we face as great a danger, as fearsome a risk, as any people in history.

Although modern equipment and improved methods have been developed that ease hiking of its drudgery and hard physical work, and open it to all ages, there is nothing new about hiking and camping with only what can be easily packed on one's back. Our early frontiersmen traveled that way whenever they entered the wilderness. Daniel Boone spent two whole years more or less alone in the virgin wilderness of Kentucky, living off the country, with no outfit except that which he had been carrying when he left. Those who have never done any backpacking in the right manner, with a good outfit, have the idea that it is the toughest kind of toil. One often hears the expression "I don't propose to make a packhorse of myself." Many who have attempted such a vacation never repeat it, because they have found it too much like hard work. Any resemblance to hard work, however, is due entirely to improper equipment and mis-

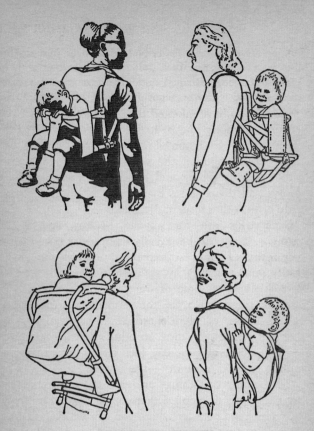

TYPICAL CHILD CARRIERS.

Across Top: A child weighing up to 50 pounds may ride facing either forward or backwards in the Hike-A-Poose which has other multiple-use features adapted to feeding, car travel, or conversion for use as a regular pack frame. (Information available from Himalayan Back Packs, P.O. Box 950, Monterey, Calif. 93940)

Across Bottom: Another child carrier is the Kiddie Pack (left) and the Kiddie Carrier (right). (Information available from either Holubar Mountaineering Ltd., P.O. Box 7, Boulder, Colo. 80302 or Gerry, Division of Outdoor Sports Industries, Inc., 5450 North Valley Highway, Denver, Colo. 80216) taken technique. Done right, there is nothing hard about vacationing with a packsack. You wander free and unfettered, with just enough exercise in the pure air to make the life thoroughly enjoyable.

Those who have adopted the best methods of backpacking, formerly known to a few, are returning regularly to the trails and bringing others with them. Many are combining the satisfaction of hiking and camping with fishing and hunting in unspoiled wilderness, all this at costs they could not even approximate in any other form of diversion.

Such trips are for anyone healthy and fairly vigorous. They can be equally enjoyed by parents, by teen-agers of both sexes, elderly people in good health, and certainly by children. One of the important sidelines of some of the packsack companies is child carriers, such as the Himalayan Industries' Hike-A-Poose, which Richard Mack has designed so that the youngster riding an adult's back, something like a papoose of yore, can face either forwards or— especially in bush country—backwards.

Today only two things are essential for backpacking vacations: drinking water, which you can purify if you must, and country where you can walk and camp without trespassing. Hikers in the United States are therefore particularly fortunate.

Open Areas for Backpacking

Within the 154 National Forests in thirty-nine states and Puerto Rico are 182,000,000 such acres and more than 105,000 miles of actual trails, all open to backpacking. National parks are crisscrossed with thousands of miles of maintained trails. Innumerable public campgrounds are enmeshed by well-marked webs of hiking paths which lead to every type of attraction. Considerable undeveloped countryside everywhere, within easy reach of even the largest cities, calls for exploration on foot.

Toting everything you need, you can rove in the woods of all our Atlantic States; in the forests of northern Michigan, Wisconsin, and Minnesota; in the Ozark Mountains; and in the pinon and cactus highlands around Taos, New Mexico—where Kit Carson made his camps earlier.

If you live near crowded New York, there are the Catskill Mountains only three hours away by car. North of Boston, beyond the inviting backways of Essex and Gloucester, are the White Mountains with the Little Imp and other unforgettable trails. Just east of Philadelphia are the South Jersey pine barrens. From the Capitol of our country, the cloud-scoured Blue Ridge is only two hours distant.

Hiking on the Long Trail

Vermont's Long Trail is a wilderness footpath for hikers. Extending from Canada to Massachusetts, it winds along or near the crest of the State's historic Green Mountains. Some ninety side trails, together with frequent crossings of country roads, provide such frequent access to supplies that it's possible to make this trip with ultralight equipment. Crisscross the route beforehand in an automobile and cache food—which can be done conveniently under rock shelves—preferably largely in cans, for easy storage and preparation. The fact that there are some sixty-three shelters, open or enclosed, along the way makes

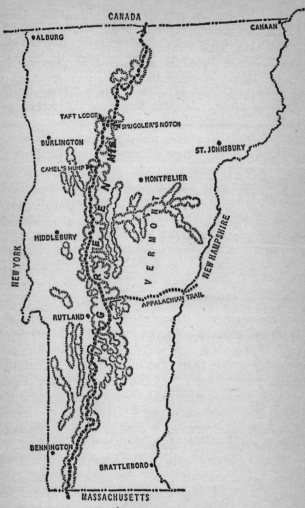

VERMONT'S 255-MILE LONG TRAIL.

Moving north, the Appalachian and Long Trails separate at a point slightly northeast of Rutland.

such a lightweight trip even more practical. These havens are never more than a day's hike apart.

The Long Trail was conceived by James P. Taylor, the Associate Principal at Vermont Academy. Mr. Taylor, who took many hiking trips with the boys of V.A., found the existing trails of the Green Mountains too few and too inadequate. After considerable preliminary work, he called a meeting in 1910 of interested individuals. Twenty-three attended, and the still thriving Green Mountain Club was formed. The next year club members built twenty-nine miles of trail, from Camel's Hump to famous Smugglers' Notch. The trail was completed from Canada to Massachusetts in 1930, and the club turned its energies to the shelter-building that is still going on.

The length of the Long Trail is a fraction over 255 miles, approximately a hundred miles longer than Vermont itself. The more than ninety side trails add another 170 miles, making a total of about 425 miles for the complete Long Trail system. Of this, the Green Mountain Club is responsible for maintaining a total of 265 miles, 175 miles of the Long Trail and 90 miles of side trails. The U. S. Forest Service is in charge of 80 miles of the Long Trail and of the largest part of the remaining side trails. The portion of the Long Trail between Vermont 100, near Sherburne Pass, and Massachusetts 2 at Blackinton is associated with the younger Appalachian Trail.

There are now over sixty shelters on the Long Trail, one for about every four miles of trail. The largest is Taft Lodge with bunks for thirty-four. The smallest is Carmel Camp, which has a capacity of four. The Green Mountain Club maintains fifty-four of these shelters. The remainder, except for two shelters that are privately owned and maintained, are kept up by the U. S. Forest Service.

If you'd like to earn the right to join the End-to-End Club of one of this country's major trails, here's a good place to start. The way to walk all these north-south footpaths is northward if possible. That way you are troubled considerably less by sun in the eyes.

Detailed information on the Long Trail is available from the Green Mountain Club, Inc., Box 94, Rutland, Vermont 05701, which puts out an up-to-date guidebook to this footpath in the wilderness for $1.50. This easily packed booklet gives the mapped, step-by-step story; some other publications are also available.

Riding and Hiking Trail

Although within recent years backpacking in the United States has been growing faster than any other major outdoor recreation, the proposed 3,000-mile California Riding and Hiking Trail will probably never be completed. This was to have extended from San Ysidro near Mexico northward through the Tehachapi Mountains and the Sierra Nevada to near the Oregon line, returning in a long loop through the breezy coast mountains. Somewhat less than 1,000 miles have been already developed, most of them along existing trails in Federal lands.

The program became impossible to finish, as matters now stand, because of the lack of funds and the inability of the state agency involved to obtain legislation giving it the right of eminent domain. Now that the original objective has been dropped, sections of the system that were feasible have been reverted to the Federal Government. In the meantime the California Department of Parks and Recreation, P. O. Box 2390, 1416 Ninth Street, Sacramento, California 95811, continues to expand trail systems in State Parks, particularly those in the larger wilderness areas.

Original Riding and Hiking Trail construction specifications called for a minimum trail width of thirty inches, to be built through a twenty-foot right-of-way. A system of overnight camps was started, the units to have been spaced some fifteen to twenty miles apart, with facilities consisting of stoves, tables, water, sanitation, and corrals. All in all, the wilderness through which the loop was planned is among the most magnificent in the West, and if you're in its vicinity with a few days to spare, you can enjoy the existing short strips of it piecemeal.

Information on the completed portions of this erstwhile trail system that are now being enthusiastically used may be obtained from the Design and Development Division of the Department of Parks and Recreation, whose address is given above, and from the U.S. Forest Service, 630 Sansome Street, San Francisco, California 94111.

The Two Big Ones . . .

Then there is the 1,995-mile footpath known as the Appalachian Trail, with its chain of free lean-tos and fireplaces, which twists from Mount Katahdin in Maine to Springer Mountain in Georgia. On the other side of the continent, the rugged 2,156-mile Pacific Crest Trail extends from Canada to Mexico in a country-long slash from near Mount Baker in

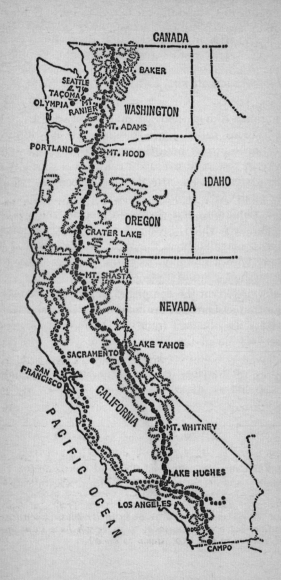

Washington to Campo in San Diego County, California. Both are enlivened by hundreds of miles of secondary trails that invite side excursions.

The Appalachian Trail

The Appalachian Trail is a free, serene, slightly incredible footpath that crosses the sparkling lake and mountain country of Maine, goes through the Green and White Mountains and the Berkshire Hills, and finally leads through the restful wild areas along the crests of the Catskill and Allegheny Mountains, Blue Ridge, and the Great Smoky to its southern terminus.

Among the feeder paths to this great wilderness thoroughfare is the Horseshoe Trail, which starts at the historic Valley Forge battlefield and joins the main Appalachian Trail at Manada Gap, Pennsylvania. The Horseshoe, unlike the parent route, is a riding lane as well as a footpath. There are also numerous motor roads that cross the summits of these mountains, thus tapping the Trail and providing easy access to it from any of the eastern states.

The wilderness way twines, for the most part, at elevations of from two to five thousand feet through high wooded mountains with many open crests. It passes through a well-watered country. There are

---

TWO FAMOUS WESTERN TRAILS.

The Pacific Crest Trail (heavy line) runs through 22 national forests. The California Riding and Hiking Trail extends north to Oregon with the Pacific Crest Trail from Campo. Near Mt. Shasta, it has a separate loop extending west and to the south near the coast and rejoining the Pacific Crest Trail near Lake Hughes. This segment is still partially under construction (see broken line) but over 1,000 miles of its length have been improved and are in use. (Not drawn to scale.)

campgrounds with fireplaces and a large number of lean-tos along it for those who do not choose to pack their own shelter. Innumerable camp spots exist everywhere for the more experienced.

Weather and travel conditions are best from about the middle of June to late September. The climate at these generally high altitudes is a relief during these months from the swelter of the lowlands—and from the noise and grime of nervous vacation traffic. Hiking and camping under close-to-arctic conditions is possible for the more strenuous during the snowy months.

Here and there along the Appalachian Trail will be found an occasional lodge and small vacation resort. As a rule, however, it is still all wilderness. Those who plan to take fullest advantage of the outdoor opportunities the country affords must pack shelter and food on their backs, as it is a hikers' route and not a horse trail.

It is unnecessary to overburden oneself with weighty equipment and food. The mild summer nights demand a minimum of bedding—except in the White Mountains areas above the timberline, where the weather is unpredictable. A very light down bag is ideal. Every three or four hiking days along the Trail there are branch paths, and sometimes roads, winding down to farming land and small villages where country stores afford a chance to replenish food supplies.

Good fishing abounds in many of the streams that splash from the crests. Much of the trail crosses national forests where hunting is permitted in season, always in conformity with state laws. Some of it passes through national parks, where fishing is permis-

THE APPALACHIAN TRAIL.

Popular with hikers, this famous trail extends from Maine to Georgia.

sible, but not hunting nor carrying firearms (unless they have been sealed or otherwise rendered inoperative).

The Appalachian Trail is a volunteer recreational project. It is supervised and maintained by the Appalachian Trail Conference, with headquarters at 1718 N Street, N.W., Washington, D.C. 20036. This is a federation of organizations, mainly outing clubs,

and individuals interested in the footpath. Its activi-
ties and objectives are entirely voluntary. Having no
salaried employees, it furnishes complete information
about the trail by means of its pamphlets, guidebooks,
bulletins, and maps. A small charge is made for these.
The funds so derived are used to republish the litera-
ture.

The Pacific Crest Trail

The Pacific Crest Trail extends from Canada to Mexico along the crests of the Cascade, Sierra Nevada,
and Sierra Madre mountains. In its country-long slash
it incorporates seven major units, largely built and
maintained by the National Park Service and the
U.S. Forest Service. These are almost entirely within
government parks and forests. Only some 160 miles,
in fact, lie outside these public lands.

The long path—skirting such famous mountains as
Ranier, Adams, Hood, Shasta, and towering Whitney
—is not a rustic lane for picnic parties. It is, in its
rugged countrywide traverse from lodgepole pine to
dusty cactus, a wilderness route for expert outdoorsmen. This does not imply that numerous scenic portions of the Trail, particularly in California, are not
entirely feasible even for families with eight-year-old
children and eighty-year-old grandparents. They are.

The Sierra Club (1050 Mills Tower, 220 Bush
Street, San Francisco, California 94104) is an orga-
nization that has done much in bringing the Pacific
Crest Trail to the attention of the public and in fos-
tering a great deal of what it stands for. Founded in
1892, with naturalist John Muir the first president, the

Sierra Club with its present thousands of members each year organizes Knapsack Trips here and elsewhere into the high hills, "offering the freedom and challenge of wilderness exploration with everything you need on your back." For details, write the Outing Department at the above address.

However, the Sierra Club is not the source of information for the Pacific Crest Trail, having no jurisdiction there nor administering the route in any way. Instead, you should write the Regional Forester at Region Six, 319 S.W. Pine Street, Portland, Oregon 97208 or at 630 Sansome Street, San Francisco, California 94111.

Much of the robust course is suitable for well-shod pack animals as well as for hikers. Most of it passes through very wild country, with considerable distances between supply points. This is higher, steeper in spots, than the Appalachian Trail. Some of it zigzags to altitudes one and two miles above sea level. Because of snow in the high country, portions are not always penetrable until at least well into July.

Only a few railroads and highways cross the main trail. All along the mountains, however, there are numerous roads entering from the lowlands. These bring you to it after one or two days of travel from main highways. Some of these side trails are, as a matter of fact, equal in scenic and recreational features to the north-south wilderness path itself. At the ends of many of these approaches will be found outfitters with pack animals and supplies for trail travel.

You can arrange, if you want, for a packer with his train to take you along the trail as far as you wish, perhaps going in over one lateral road and coming out along another. The more popular plan though, when you aren't going to do all the walking, is to have an outfitter pack your duffle into a more or less permanent camp in some favorably situated locality and then pick you up later on some prearranged date. In the meantime you can explore the region with a backpack. The country is so vast, and in most areas the scenery is so varied, that you can easily spend a month or more taking short trips from an established camp and never exhaust the possibilities for new experiences and enjoyment.

The Pacific Crest Trail is the roughest of the four. Also, the nights there are apt to be cooler than on the East's Appalachian Trail and Long Trail. In the West, therefore—depending of course on where you hike— some of your equipment may well approach that of the Alpinist. Strong mountain shoes, preferably with cleated rubber soles that will cut through gravel and give you sure footing on rocks, are highly desirable. You'll probably appreciate a warm jacket, shirt, or sweater for the evenings. Bedding in general should be a little heavier than along the Atlantic heights of the continent. A down sleeping bag, a mummy type weighing not over five pounds, will be excellent.

Along neither route is a regular tent essential during moderate weather. A compact plastic poncho, weighing less than a pound, will pinch-hit perfectly for both raincoat and shelter.

A compass is always desirable. Although the main wilderness trails are well marked, it is easy to get mixed up on directions in the haze and clouds often encountered at high altitudes.

Obtaining Good Maps

Good maps are in general extraordinarily easy to obtain. Even the small-scale maps distributed free by gasoline stations and automobile clubs give a general picture. The trail organizations mentioned sometimes have available extremely detailed maps of their routes, with almost step-by-step directions in some of their accompanying guidebooks.

Sectional maps, particularly those governmental publications which are sold below cost, are very inexpensive. Most suppliers will furnish upon request free detailed lists of what they have available. One of these is the Superintendent of Documents, U. S. Government Printing Office, Washington, D.C. 20402.

Maps of the portions of the United States east of the Mississippi River may be obtained from the U. S. Geological Survey, Washington, D.C. 20242. Maps of areas west of the Mississippi are available from the U. S. Geological Survey, Federal Center, Denver, Colorado 80225. Topographic maps of National Park areas are also available from the Map Information Office here.

Canadian maps may be secured from provincial publicity offices located in the various province capitals, from the Government Travel Bureau in Ottawa, and from the Map Distribution Office, Department of Mines and Technical Surveys, which is also located in Ottawa, Ontario.

For governmental maps of Mexico, write to Dirección de Geografia y Meteorologia, Tacubaya, D. F., Mexico. Two private sources for foreign maps are: (1) the National Geographic Society, 1145 17th Street, N.W., Washington, D.C. 20036; and (2) the

International Map Company, 595 Broad Avenue, Ridgefield, N.J. 07657.

The best Pacific Crest Trail maps are those of the national forests published by the U. S. Forest Service, Washington, D.C. 20250. If you will specify the particular sections of the trail in which you are interested, this office of Agriculture will tell you what maps are available for the area and how much they cost.

The supervisors of the various forests can furnish both planimetric maps of their areas and the names of outfitters in the regions. The two U. S. Forest Service regional headquarter offices covering the Pacific Crest Trail area are located at 630 Sansome Street, San Francisco, California 94111 and in the Post Office Building, Portland, Oregon 97208.

Contour maps, when available, are by far the most valuable for hiking use, because they indicate valleys, canyons, mountains, and other such geographical features in terms of elevation. Consulting such a map in a strange country can save one an exhausting amount of unnecessary climbing, descending, and then climbing again. Forest Service maps rarely include contours. If you are interested in contour maps, therefore, contact the U. S. Geological Survey, Washington, D. C. 20242. They publish free index sheets of individual states, and from these you can determine whether the topographic maps you want are available.

More National Scenic Trails

In pace with the unprecedented surge of country-wide backpacking fervor, a pleasure which during the past few years has grown faster than any other major outdoor recreation activity, Congress has designated fourteen other routes for study and possible inclusion in the National Trails System. These are:

(1) Continental Divide Trail, a 3,100-mile path extending from near the Mexican border in southwestern New Mexico northward, generally along the Continental Divide, to the Canadian border in Glacier National Park.

(2) Potomac Heritage Trail, an 825-mile route extending generally from the mouth of the Potomac River to its sources in West Virginia, including the ancient 70-mile Chesapeake and Ohio Canal towpath.

(3) Old Cattle Trails of the Southwest from the vicinity of San Antonio, Texas, approximately 800 miles through Oklahoma via Baxter Springs and Chetopa, Kansas, to Fort Scott, Kansas, including the Chisholm Trail, from the vicinity of San Antonio or Cuero, Texas, approximately 800 miles north through Oklahoma to Abilene, Kansas.

(4) Lewis and Clark Trail from Wood River, Illinois, to Oregon's Pacific Ocean, following routes of the Lewis and Clark expedition.

(5) Natchez Trace, from Nashville, Tennessee, approximately 600 miles to Natchez, Mississippi.

(6) North Country Trail, from the Appalachian Trail in Vermont, approximately 3,200 miles through the States of New York, Pennsylvania, Ohio, Michigan, Wisconsin, and Minnesota, to the Lewis and Clark Trail in North Dakota.

(7) Kittanning Trail from Shirleysburg in Huntingdon County, Pennsylvania, to Kittanning, Armstrong County, Pennsylvania.

(8) Oregon Trail, from Independence, Missouri,

approximately 2,000 miles to near historic Fort Van-
cover, Washington.

(9) Santa Fe Trail, from Independence, Missouri,
approximately 800 sun-beaten miles to Santa Fe, New
Mexico.

(10) Long Trail, extending a bit more than 255
miles from the Massachusetts border northward
through green Vermont to the Canadian border.

(11) Mormon Trail, extending from Nauvoo, Illinois, to Salt Lake City, Utah, through the States of
Iowa, Nebraska, and Wyoming.

(12) Gold Rush Trails in Alaska, including the
path over stirring Chilkoot Pass.

(13) Mormon Battalion Trail, reaching 2,000 miles
from Mount Pisgah, Iowa, through Kansas, Colorado,
New Mexico, and Arizona to Los Angeles, California.

(14) El Camino Real from St. Augustine to Fort
Caroline National Memorial, Florida, approximately
30 scenic miles along the southern boundary of the
St. Johns River.

The U.S. Bureau of Outdoor Recreation in coopera-
tion with the Forest Service and other Federal as
well as State and local agencies is already working
on this vast plan, studies of which are expected to be
completed by 1976, the Nation's 200th anniversary.
Up-to-the-minute information on current developments along any of these luring bypaths may be
secured by writing the Bureau of Outdoor Recreation,
Department of the Interior, Washington, D.C. 20240.

As J. E. Jensen, Associate Director of the National
Park Service, so aptly tells me:

We realize that in order for man to increase his awareness of the natural environment he must have contact with
it. And through such experiences as hiking in the back

country he can find solitude, inspiration, and aesthetic enjoyment, all contributing to his awareness. Therefore, in order to preserve this unique experience for all generations, present and future, we must maintain those natural phenomena inherent in a given area. Although we cannot shut down these places, we all can restrict our use in those areas now available and strive to obtain additional ones in order to shift the load.

One such plan is to acquire parks and recreational lands near our urban centers. And we are presently doing this. This move would not only allow more people a chance to obtain a park experience but would also reduce travel requirements and lessen the impact on previously established areas.

Appropriate Backpack Weights

To travel the routes we have discussed, and explore the regions adjacent to them, an easily carried outfit containing equipment and food for each person is indispensable. For backpacking, everything should be cut down in weight and bulk to the absolute essentials. Food should be largely dehydrated.

Briefly, the total weight of the backpack for mountain travel should not exceed about thirty-five pounds for young and strenuous men. This maximum should be pared down to some fifteen to twenty-five pounds for juniors and women. As for proportions, the equipment proper in the largest pack should not weigh over fifteen pounds—thus allowing a food load of at least twenty pounds. In these days of lightweight grub, one can take off for a month at a time. And even this time can be stretched when rations are supplemented with wild edibles, like fish and berries, as one goes along.

And so at the end of the paved road—you shoulder your pack and head into the country. You leave a lot of hustle and bustle—and expenses—behind. There's no other kind of vacation that can compare to these backpacking trips, none that can take you quite so close to peace and utter freedom.

2/Taking Your Pick of the Packs

as a binding material, or they lay on all bare surfaces away from the back. Carrying bags obtainable from the same source fit on the frames. The result is utility

2

Available Types of Packs

Only two packs are really satisfactory for this sort of vacation. One is the alpine type of frame rucksack, usually with a single large and several smaller fabric compartments built around a strong, light, metal frame to which shoulder straps are fastened. The other is the packboard, basically a rectangular frame over which fabric is so tightly doubled and laced that a bundle lashed to it never touches the hiker's back. Both are obtainable in different sizes.

The best packs in the world for this type of recreation are variations of the packboard made in the United States and available in stores throughout the country.

Light, strong, and durable, such packboards are usually made of tough aluminum tubing, although such metals as magnesium and stainless steel are also used. Webbing, usually nylon, keeps all hard surfaces away from the back. "Carrying bags" obtainable from the same sources fit on the frames. The result is utility plus convenience and comfort. Anyone planning to cover very many miles of recreational backpacking would do well, everything else being equal, to make

such a pack the basic part of his outfit. The wrong
pack has ruined more vacations than any other single
item.

Alpine Frame Rucksack

The packs just described are, in their present forms,
essentially American—although they evolved from
the primitive backpacking experience among the Indians and peoples the world over.

The alpine type of frame rucksack is a European
development. It largely replaced the packboard there.
This is in part because of fashion, but it's also the
result of the low center of gravity enjoyed by such
frame rucksacks as the Bergans variety, which makes
them particularly adapted to such prime European
sports as climbing and skiing. In recent years, however, the American packboards have been making
increasing inroads in Europe.

Frame rucksacks are indeed extremely comfortable
with light loads. Their multipocketed sacks, the utility of which is widely recognized by the American
packers, are certainly handy when you want to get at
various parts of the load without unpacking the whole
outfit. Besides dividing the sack into convenient compartments, these partitions also help the sack to keep
its functional shape. The rucksacks' design, with the
top of the sack hanging away from the back, makes
them cool and keeps the point of gravity low.

The latter characteristic becomes a disadvantage,
however, when heavy loads are carried. The back-
ward tilt of the sack then becomes a drag on the hips
and legs, at the same time pulling the body off balance. In fact, I found when first using this type of

pack that my tendency was to compensate by reaching back with one hand and pulling forward on the top strap. This not only immobilizes one arm, but it interferes with one's natural rhythm and heats up the upper back. Another disadvantage of this pack with

BERGAN-MEIS FRAME PACK.

A comfortable imported pack originating in Norway. Bag is mounted on a light tubular-steel framework, bow-shaped at the bottom. (Abercrombie and Fitch, N.Y.C.)

LIGHTWEIGHT RUCKSACK FOR DAY TRIPS.

Weighing only 2¼ pounds, this rucksack has a light metal frame and a sack size 12" x 14" x 5"—a typical rucksack adapted to short trips.

heavy loads is its increased tendency to sway, further disrupting the balance.

Frame rucksacks, then, are functional for ordinary trail carrying for pleasure only when the loads are relatively light. Lightness of course is a relative thing, being largely in ratio with an individual's own body weight. On the average, it might be generalized that the Bergans type of frame rucksack is not the best choice for day after day of trail packing when the load is more than about twenty-five pounds.

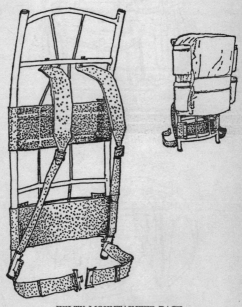

KELTY MOUNTAINEER PACK.

A comfortable energy-conserving posture can be maintained for long-distance heavy packing with this Kelty model. (Kelty Mountaineering and Backpacking, 1801 Victory Blvd., Glendale, Calif. 91201)

Ordinary Packboards

The usual loads carried during backpacking vacations are more comfortably supported the length of the back, rather than hanging away from it, and with the center of gravity over the hips. A pack frame, either with a convenient sack or with the fabric-wrapped load attached to the frame itself, is therefore recommended. It's true that the ordinary outfit will lighten as you eat your way along the trail. But experience

TRAILWISE CONTOUR FRAME WITH PACK BAG.

Contour plus taper make this a suitable pack for an extended outing. Its full nylon mesh back further distributes weight and allows maximum air circulation between pack and wearer. (The Ski Hut, 1615 University Ave., Berkeley, Calif. 94703)

has shown that it is most practical to buy a pack for the heaviest loads that are to be carried in it.

The packboard frame, either with a solid backing such as canvas or with several large fabric bands top and bottom, will hold the properly packed load comfortably the length of the back and not just against the lower part. The best sacks, when one of these is used, are designed so that the outfit will be packed close to the body and high. Then leaning slightly forward places the center of the weight directly above the hips, where it can be balanced with the least physical exertion.

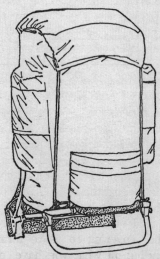

HIMALAYAN BACK PACK.

Professional quality combination featuring the famous Everest pack frame used to assault Mt. Everest. (Himalayan Back Packs, P.O. Box 950, Cannery Row, Monterey, Calif. 93940)

The arrangement of the straps and the other components of this type of pack all combine to keep the weight so centered. But the pack still must be carefully packed. With too high a load you tire yourself in all but the most even terrain, by constantly shifting the muscles to regain balance. A load with the weight too far back will drag backwards on the shoulders.

The Alaskan Packboard

Another type of packboard that has been found eminently satisfactory is the Alaskan variety. The basis of this is a rectangular frame of wood or some other rigid material about fifteen inches wide by thirty inches long, over which a canvas is doubled and tautly laced. There is about a two-and-one-half inch space between the two expanses of canvas, which—because only one surface of canvas rests against the back—insures a free circulation of air. The effect is exactly as though you were lying on your back on a canvas cot.

There are two cross members to this frame, the top being about six inches below the top of the form. To it are attached, closely together, the two broad shoulder straps. These pass through a slit in the canvas on the side toward the back. Their lower ends are fastened to the lower outside corners of the frame.

Your outfit and food are tightly wrapped in a tarpaulin or other covering so as to form a compact bundle, depending on what you have, perhaps some fifteen inches in diameter and about thirty inches long. This is lashed to the outside of the packboard. Because the load does not touch the back at all, being

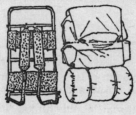

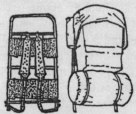

FEATURES OF A MODERN BACKPACK SYSTEM.

(Leisure Group, Inc., Union Bank Square, Fifth and Figueroa Streets, Los Angeles, Calif. 90017)

held away by the space between the two coverings of canvas, you can pack anything from a sack of fossils to an outboard motor without chafing or bruising.

The packboard should have its shoulder straps so adjusted that it sags just enough to rest some of the weight on the hips. The shoulder straps will then bear straight down on the top of the shoulders instead of pulling them uncomfortably backwards.

The commercial model of this type of pack, known as the Trapper Nelson packboard, can be obtained from almost all dealers in camp equipment. Three sizes are now made. The medium size, with a 26-inch by 14½-inch frame, is right for the average hiker. The small size, 24 inches by 13 inches, is excellent for women and youths. There is also a large size for heavy work, 30 inches by 14½ inches.

It can be had with a large canvas dunnage bag that laces to the frame. For lightweight packing with this type of pack, though, it is only extra weight. If you are going to get that sort of pack, it is generally best to obtain it without the bag and to tie on your outfit in a cover that has some other use, such as shelter, and so pays for its weight and bulk.

The army used a similar packboard for heavy mountain carrying in World War II. This is strongly and substantially made over a fiberboard frame. Some can still be found in surplus stores. Although excellent for the stress of military use, these are unnecessarily heavy for backpacking vacations.

Make Your Own Packboard

If you'd like the fun of a personal project, or have to fit packs to a family and could use the resulting savings elsewhere, it's possible to build your own packboard of this type.

Procure some strips of Sitka spruce, oak, or other strong wood, 2¼ inches wide by ½ inch thick. Cut two strips 28 inches long for the sides of the frame. Round the top ends, but leave the bottom ends square.

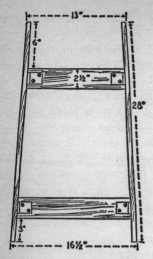

FIGURE 1. *Making Your Own Packboard—Frame Dimensions and Layout.*

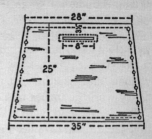

FIGURE 2. *Layout for the Packboard Cover.*

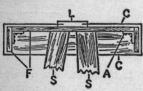

FIGURE 3. *Cover Installation—Top Cross Section. F-Wooden frame. A-Angle iron (or aluminum angle strips for less weight). C-Canvas cover. L-Lacing. S-Shoulder straps.*

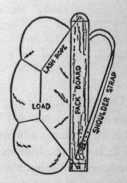

FIGURE 4. *Side View—Shoulder Straps Installed.*

Cut two other strips for the crosspieces, one 12 inches long and the other 15½ inches long. Join the two side pieces by the two crosspieces, making a

frame as shown in Figure 1. The top of the upper
crosspiece should come 6 inches down from the top
ends of the side pieces. The bottom of the lower
crosspiece should be 3 inches above the bottom ends
of the side pieces.

The edge of the side pieces and the flat of the
crosspieces face the packer's back. Notice that the
crosspieces are flush with the edge of the side pieces
farthest from the packer's back.

The crosspieces must be fastened to the side pieces
very accurately and strongly. Use angle irons with
wood screws in both faces of the irons. Any machinist
or blacksmith can make these bent pieces of metal
in a few minutes.

The resulting frame will be 13 inches wide at the
top, 16½ inches wide at the bottom, 28 inches high,
and 2½ inches thick. Using the same proportions,
you can design as many different sizes as you need.
Children, as well as adults, find these packs very
rugged and comfortable. When the youngest member
of the family finally outgrows his, it can be passed
along to some other young hiker.

Over this frame you lace a cover of, say, twelve-
ounce canvas, cut and made as shown in Figure 2.
This is, in this instance, 28 inches wide at the top,
35 inches at the bottom, and 25 inches high. It covers
the frame to within 1½ inches of the top and bottom.

Hem it all around and insert seven brass grommets
along each side edge to accommodate the lacing.
These grommets, along with inexpensive tools for inserting them, are obtainable from many sporting
goods stores and from all tent and awning makers.
The latter two, as well as some outfitters, will insert

them for a few cents if you prefer. On the side edge,
hem the cover with two folds, fastening the grommets through both folds so they won't pull out.

Three and one-half inches down from the center
of the top edge there should be a horizontal slit, 8
inches long, strongly reinforced at the edges. This is
for the shoulder straps to pass through.

This canvas cover is laced around the frame, drum
tight, by means of strong cod line passed through the
grommets. The slit comes on the side toward the
packer's back. The lacing is done on the side of the
frame where the crosspieces are flush with the edges
of the side pieces (see Figure 3). The edges with the
grommets should not meet by about 2 inches, so that
the canvas can be laced very tightly.

It should be mentioned in passing that some packers do away with the canvas entirely, lacing these
and similar frames with long cord zigzagged back
and forth through holes drilled about an inch apart
along the sidepieces. This decreases the weight and
increases the coolness, but the result is not so stable
as canvas and will not hold up under heavier loads.

The upper ends of the shoulder straps are secured
around the top crosspieces of the frame at the center.
They pass through the slit in the canvas, then around
and over the packer's shoulders, and finally are secured to the outside of the side pieces of the frame
six inches above the lower ends of these members, as
shown in Figure 4. A piece of leather with a one-inch
buckle is screwed to each of the side pieces for this
purpose.

The straps are best made of heavy chrome-tanned
leather saturated with Neatsfoot oil. They should be

2 inches wide at the top and where they go over the shoulders, tapering to an inch wide at the bottom where they are secured to the buckles. Too wide a strap passing along the armpits causes chafing. Holes are punched in the straps to provide for adjustment in length. If you will install these straps with the smooth side of the leather contacting the shoulders, the pack will be easier to slip on and off.

These days a firm, wide nylon webbing is available, both in surplus stores and from outfitters, that can be tapered for the installation of buckles. Such webbing is excellent for use as straps. In either event you will probably appreciate the use of shoulder pads, available so inexpensively that it's hardly worthwhile to bother trying to sew them at home. In a pinch, something such as heavy gloves shoved between strap and shoulder will make all the difference.

After the straps have been adjusted for length, they can most conveniently be slipped over the shoulders just as one puts on coat or suspenders. If you are alone and no elevated surface such as a stump or log is available, merely stand the loaded pack board upright on the ground. Sit down and place your arms through the straps. Run your thumbs under the straps to make sure they lie flatly on the shoulders. Then stand up.

Figure 3 shows a section of this packboard as viewed looking down from the top. Figure 4 presents a side view, with the shoulder straps in position and with a load lashed onto the board. For this, holes are drilled in the top and bottom of the sidepieces of the frame through which to attach the lashing ropes.

The Use of Tump Lines

Tump lines and backpacking vacations don't really go together. The tump line—whereby part of the weight is supported by the head or forehead, by means of a wide band which is attached to the load by two lines —is common to primitive freighting. In canoe country too, where portages are seldom as long as a mile, the tump line is common, often supporting one or more tarp-wrapped bundles or taking part of the weight of a large frameless pack, such as the Duluth, off the shoulders.

But such a pack heats and galls the back after an hour or more of packing. With head and neck immobilized by tump line, you cannot look around, enjoy the scenery, nor even properly survey the country ahead to pick out the best way. Your eyes are glued to the portage trail, and for the time being you are just a beast of burden with the tump line a tight band over your head.

For freighting uses the tump line has shown its worth over the centuries. But when you're out for a good time, you shouldn't be laden with a load heavy enough to require the use of a tump line.

A *waist belt*, however, weighing only some three ounces or so, can be welcome when you are starting out with a heavier-than-usual pack. It helps both by stabilizing the load and by transferring some of the weight from the shoulders to the slope of the buttocks.

How to Stow the Outfit

With loads changing constantly as food is used, packing is a matter of day-by-day ingenuity. It should be emphasized that packing always remains pretty much an individual affair. In other words, experiment until you find out what arrangement suits you best.

There are certain general fundamentals, however, that may serve as a basis for your trials. These differ somewhat, depending on the country. For example, too high a load will work against you in two ways if you have to do much climbing. First, it's easy to overbalance in strenuous going, and such a load under these circumstances will leave you tired out just from trying to keep it balanced. Secondly, when a load is packed high under such circumstances, it's difficult to get your head back to see where you're going.

The ideal, again, is to keep the weight tight to the body and comparatively high. The light sleeping bag, then, will probably go at the bottom, either in the sack or wrapped separately below it. The lighter objects will graduate up from the bottom and will be

Weights of Items in a Basic Pack

	POUNDS	OUNCES
Pack	3	12
Plastic tarp and poncho	1	5
Sleeping Bag	3	8
Cooking utensils	1	12
First aid kit		4
Underwear and socks		12
Wool shirt, jacket, or sweater	1	8
Toilet articles		8
Knife, whetstone		8
Flashlight		15
Needles, thread, buttons, personals		4
Total weight without food	15	

placed at the front of the pack to press the heavier impediments toward your back.

That's really about all there is to it. Personal trials will do the rest. A couple more things. The load should ordinarily be packed so that it's narrow enough not to interfere with the natural swing of the arms. And flat objects should be placed at the very back, so that parts of the load will not prod the spine.

In a party of two or more, the cooking utensils and first aid kit will be used in common, each individual carrying his share. Add a plate, cup, and spoon to cooking utensils for each additional hiker.

3/How About the Nights?

3

Selecting Your Sleeping Bag

The sleeping bag, next to the pack itself, is the most important piece of equipment to be selected for a backpacking vacation—especially as it is the most expensive item. You can bull along the trail with a poor pack. But the sleeping bag, in which you're going to be spending on the average a third of every day, has to be adequate if you're going to keep refreshed enough to keep enjoying yourself under full steam.

In really cold weather a poor bag can actually be dangerous. If you are going to be hiking in mild weather, you have a wider choice. A roomier bag can be picked. Styling, such as provisions to keep the top around the head in frosty going, can be overlooked. The way the filler is held in place, even the filler itself, will be less important. Ideally, though, any bag you buy should be the most functional obtainable, as anything less than this will mean additional bulk and weight to carry.

In the mild weather enjoyed along many trails in the summer vacation season, mistaken choices will be felt most in the pocketbook and on the shoulders.

There is considerably less latitude in really cold weather. Suppose your sleeping bag has to do for both? Then gauge your selection to fit the severest weather to be encountered.

Preserving Body Warmth

No sleeping bag produces any warmth by itself. In the absence of a fire, the body is ordinarily the only heat-generating machine in a trail camp.

The average adult hiker, sleeping or lounging relaxed beside a campfire, liberates somewhat less than a hundred calories of heat every hour. This output can be increased in two ways. Rigorous exertion can, over the day, multiply the yield as much as six times. Even shivering—a form of muscular exercise, and one of nature's safeguards against freezing—will build up the release of body warmth several times. Eating also stimulates the caloric output. The increase is quicker, although of shorter duration, with carbohydrates; greater and more lasting with proteins.

The skin automatically begins to shut off surface blood circulation when exposed to cold. It can thus decrease the heat loss from the skin by as much as a fourth of normal loss. Alcohol, it so happens, prevents this natural thermostat from functioning properly, at the same time bringing about such rapid and sometimes dangerous heat losses that the backpacker may be deluded into believing himself warmed and stimulated. Wind, as well as low temperature, produces chilling and accelerated dissipation of body warmth.

All that a sleeping bag or any other bedding can do is delay the loss of body warmth by insulating the individual both against undue waste of that heat and against encroachment of cold and wind. Incidentally, these cannot maintain heat balance at subzero temperatures except when the body has some of its stored heat to spare.

The most effective insulation known is dry, still air. Thus the effectiveness of bed materials in keeping one warm is in direct proportion, not to their weight, but to the number of dead air cells they can maintain. The thicker a sleeping robe or blanket is and the fluffier its nature, the more inert air it affords.

Sleeping Bag Materials

Not too many years ago, sleeping bags consisted of several thicknesses of wool blankets sewn in bag form inside an outer sack of canvas. They were little else, in fact, than a more or less convenient and controversial way of preventing one from kicking off the blankets during sleep. The better modern sleeping bags utilize far more effective insulating materials, which are at once thicker and lighter than blankets, affording considerably more dead air space pound for pound.

It will take a sleeping bag about one and three-fourths inches thick to keep you warm when the thermometer has dropped around the freezing mark. Another quarter-inch of thickness will be required for each additional ten degrees of coldness. An easy way to measure thickness, by the way, is to fluff up the bag, open it, and spread it out on a table. Lay a piece of cardboard flat across the top. Then measure between it and the table.

Insulation being a question of thickness rather than one of weight, the most perfect insulation—taking

flexibility and heft into consideration—is made up of
small layers of dead air. Actually, when these lamina-
tions of air are controlled, they approach their peak
of effectiveness when they are a quarter of an inch
thick. (Greater widths of dead air tend to lose heat,
because of tiny convective currents.) Caused by air
rising on the warm side of the air cell and settling
along the cold side of the cell, these set up a circulation that quickly increases the rate of heat exchange
between the two walls of the insulative material.

The most nearly ideal insulating material, for use
in sleeping bags and in cold-weather clothing, is to be
found in the delicate down of birds. This down varies
even among the same species of birds. Generally
speaking, the finest grade of down available commercially is the very best white goose down. There is also
a lower grade, which is no warmer than the best of
grey goose down. Other goose down is next, followed
by prime duck down. Still other downs follow, trailed
by a mixture of down and feathers, and then by
feathers themselves.

Thickness, again, determines the amount of warmth
obtainable. Laboratory experiments have shown that
this is true whether the insulative material is steel
wool or kapok. For a sleeping bag, of course, steel
wool is out of the question. Kapok, a vegetable fiber,
is not really suitable for a hiking bag. It is both heavy
and unstable, deteriorating to powder with continued
use.

As a matter of fact, the next thing to downs and
feathers in thermal value—and the thing to consider
if the family on a budget is going on a backpacking
vacation in mild weather—is dacron. This is very
satisfactory under such circumstances, and the filler

is extremely durable. But you are paying for the difference in cost by taking on added pounds and bulk. For backpacking trips where functional weight is very important, it is not advisable to pick up any of the less expensive sleeping bags, although many are on the market. The bag is so important that it would be advisable to make any necessary savings elsewhere—perhaps by passing up the new lightweight simplicities in the food line and relying, for a while at least, on the old-fashioned staples.

Choosing Your Mummy Bag

In addition to its compactness and lightness, there are two reasons for selecting a mummy bag for your backpacking vacation. First of all, the volume of the bag which must be heated by the body is kept at a minimum. Secondly, the surface area of the bag through which this heat is lost is likewise kept as small as possible. Therefore you have the warmest arrangement that is available.

Some individuals take immediately to these form-fitting bags. In my own case, they took some getting used to. But nearly everyone who seriously tries one comes to like it, especially if the interior is made of some slick fabric such as nylon, which makes for the most ease of movement and rapidly adjusts to body temperature on even the coldest nights.

There are those go-light hikers who look upon such a sleeping bag as an extra garment to be worn at night; they move the whole tightly fitting contrivance with them when they turn. There is nothing wrong with this practice. In fact a few things are in its favor, if it doesn't roll you off the mattress. I prefer a bag, though, that's at least large enough so that you can get in the habit of pressing it downward with your arms and then maneuvering enough with your hips and legs to hold it while you shift position.

There are several factory methods of arranging the filler in such bags, each with its advantages. One characteristic that all good mummy bags should have, however, is a differential cut whereby the inner bag, even when expanded, does not compress the insulation against the outer cover and thus decrease its warmth. The outer cover of bags cut this way will look and feel loose.

Awnings and Pockets

A number of sleeping bags are provided with an awning attached to the cover; this awning can be erected as a shelter over the head. Advertising agencies delight in picturing sleeping bags with the awning raised and the hiker sleeping blissfully in a downpour of rain. It is a provocative selling point, undeniably.

The difficulty on the actual trail is that any such sleeping bag would have to be waterproof, and this would be an impractical arrangement. In warm weather, no matter how dry, sleeping in such a bag would be like drowsing in a steam bath. In cold temperatures, the imprisoned body moisture would soon counteract all insulating qualities and hasten freezing. You need to sleep under a tarpaulin, tent, or some other shelter in stormy weather.

The air mattress pockets provided on the bottom sides of sleeping bags by some manufacturers are neither necessary nor advisable. They add weight and expense. At best, they are nuisances—just something else to wear out. And employing them means that you will not be able to use the bag equally on both sides. Alternating the top and bottom, as is possible with sleeping bags opening down one side, will add both to the article's longevity and to your comfort.

Furthermore, there is absolutely no need for a mattress pocket. The reason some individuals are troubled for awhile by a bed's slipping off its pneumatic softener is usually that the latter has been blown up too hard.

Using an Air Mattress

Maximum comfort is attained when one has an air mattress under a good, adequate sleeping bag. One of these requires only a minute or so to inflate properly. In contrast, a browse mattress—available only in real wilderness—requires about half an hour to make, and then it mats down enough to be uncomfortably hard after the second night.

The natural tendency among individuals accustomed to sleeping on the rather solid conventional bed is to blow their air mattresses too full. It will be just about right if you inflate it so that when you stretch out on your side, your hip bone just about touches the hard surface beneath. The easiest way to accomplish this at first is by deliberately overinflating, then lying in position and adjusting by opening the valve until the desired pressure is reached.

For backpacking, where weight and space are primary considerations, a good air mattress to secure is one about four feet long and half as wide. This should be located beneath the two vulnerable points as far as sleeping comfort is concerned, the shoulders and the hips. Browse, leaves, brush, or anything else suitable (such as the pack itself) may then be used to level off under the legs.

The stability afforded by this last leveling-off of the sleeping surface generally eliminates any tendency there may be to roll off the mattress during the night. Once the average individual has slept on such an arrangement for several nights, he won't have any trouble in making his bed stay put. Most people, unless they fall into the trap of overinflation, never do experience any difficulty.

All air mattresses are admittedly cold in frosty weather. Although it's true that they do provide insulation from ground dampness, the air within stays at just about the surrounding temperature. Best solution during backpacking vacations in cold weather? Spread as much clothing as you can between the mattress and the bed. This cold-weather disadvantage is more than offset by the coolness afforded during the hot months by having nothing more substantial beneath you than a mass of air.

Any air mattress should be laid on a hard, flat, rigid surface. There is no need to bother removing minor irregularities such as small roots. The mattress will automatically adjust to them, although with some of the more fragile models you have to use care to prevent scraping and puncturing. Always carry a small repair kit in any event.

One occasionally sees these mattresses being used on sagging bunks in hiking shelters, to the discomfort of the occupants. Sleeping on the floor under such conditions is far more relaxing. A sagging bunk can be adapted to air mattress use, however, by providing it with a solid surface of boards or poles.

Redistributing the Down

One difficulty experienced with sleeping bags in which down and feather fillers are used is that this insulation has a tendency to shift towards the bottom. This leaves the upper area of the robe vulnerable to low temperatures. In some instances it results in the expense and nuisance of returning the article to the factory for renovation.

You can redistribute the filler on the spot, as a matter of fact. The process is very simple. Open the article if possible. Lay it on a hard surface, such as the ground or floor, with the inside upward. Procure a supple stick about a yard long. Then start beating the robe lightly from the foot up toward the top. You will be able to feel when a reasonably uniform thickness has been restored. If necessary, turn the robe over and go through the same process on the other side.

Adjusting the Warmth

It is usually wisest when possible to choose a sleeping robe suitable for the lowest temperatures you expect to encounter on your hike. A good down robe that will keep you cozy on subzero nights in the mountains can still be pleasant in the warmth of summer lowlands.

By that time you will be using it nearly open; and

you will probably be sleeping with at least your head, arms, and shoulders uncovered. A robe with snaps, preferable anyway to the heavy and vulnerable zipper for wilderness use, can be better adjusted to changing temperatures.

The warmth of a down bag, and to a lesser extent that of all bags, can be regulated to a very large degree by the frequency with which it is aired. In very cold going, daily airings will keep the down fluffed out and the heat-absorbing moisture expelled. When you get up, too, open the bag and pump out the moist air. Better still, turn the bag inside out. After unpacking at night, fluff up the filler.

In hot weather you'll find the bag more comfortable, though somewhat heavier, if it is aired only as it lies on the bed. Incidentally, care should be taken when a robe is hung over a line to suspend it, if possible, parallel to the tubes that contain the insulation.

Using Hood Arrangements

The tendency is to pull the head under the covers in really cold weather. This should never be done, however, because the moisture in one's breath then tends to build up in the bag, decreasing its warmth.

Hood arrangements are available on the better cold-weather bags. The head may thus be warmly enclosed when the sap in the trees starts freezing. If the nose gets too cold, cover it with a woolen shirt. But the nose always remains out.

When it gets this cold, incidentally, take the flashlight into the bag with you—or at least shove it under one side. Extreme coldness may immobilize the batteries.

Zippers versus Snaps

You may select a bag with a zipper; many of the very
finest sleeping bags now on the market have this convenient type of closure. If you do, be very careful of
this fastener. The bags with zippers frequently de-
velop trouble, sometimes jamming entirely and per-
manently, and in other cases requiring excessive
maneuvering every time they have to be opened or
shut.

Zippers also tend to mean lost heat. They can be
insulated; but this increases the likelihood of snagging, which can be a considerable nuisance. When
snagging is guarded against by suitable webbing fac-
ins, a heavy assembly is the result. As far as that goes,
the zipper itself, especially if it is installed so that the
bag opens flat, quickly builds up added weight.

Even with zippers of the present sturdy construction, one must proceed with care. When a slide fastener snags, it's a bad idea to tug or yank at it.
Instead, take a close look and try to find the trouble.
If a fold of fabric is pinched in the track, unzip the
fastener about an inch, smooth out the fabric, hold it
out of the way with a finger, and try again. When
the slide fastener works stiffly, rub a thin lubricating
coat of wax or lead-pencil graphite on each side of
the track and work the fastener open and shut a few
times.

Snaps are often used instead of zippers for fastening bags, and over the years I have much preferred
these. In cold weather they have the advantage of
eliminating the cold seam through which a zipper is
always stitched. In warm weather, they can be
opened here and there so that the bag will have a

highly adjustable system of ventilation. Finally, they almost never get out of order—and even if one should go, the overlap between the two on either side of it will be sufficient to keep you sleeping in comfort.

Warmer Without Clothing

The warmest practical way to sleep is to get a bag that's heavy enough and then strip down to no more than shorts or light pajamas. Even at best, wearing any clothing in a bag picks up body moisture and interferes with the circulation. The Eskimo, whose personal experience teaches him the most effectual ways of adjusting to the cold, prefers to sleep nude.

Except for something to protect your feet, you won't need to put on anything if you have to haul out for any reason. The body will retain its own aura of warmth for a couple of minutes or so. Such exposure will not be harmful in any respect, nor even unpleasant. You'll probably be shivering when you crawl back into the sack; but the warmth will soon come, and its influence will be so relaxing that almost at once you'll be drowsing again.

The place that your clothing will do the most good is between the bag and the mattress, serving as additional insulation. This is especially true if you are using an air mattress.

Drying Your Clothing

Damp clothing taken into the sleeping bag will be largely dried by body heat. There are great disadvantages to this practice if it is at all overdone, however. For one thing, heat is consumed that otherwise would go to keeping the body warm, and this may make you cold, especially since your metabolism is at its lowest ebb. For another thing, much of the moisture is picked up by the bag itself, increasing its weight and decreasing its warmth. Finally, it's uncomfortable to have any amount of damp clothing in the bag with you.

The best procedure, when at all possible, is to dry the clothing in the warmth of a shelter stove or a crackling campfire. When this cannot be done, it may be just as well to be philosophical about the whole thing. If the clothing is the right sort, it will only be clammy and really uncomfortable when you first put it on in the morning. In any event, dripping shrubbery along the trail will very likely soon get it wet again.

Providing For a Pillow

You may find that some sort of pillow will add to your comfort. This may be a folded shirt. If you've ounces to spare, it may be a small pillow case that you can stuff daily with dry pine needles or wild marsh hay. It may be an air pillow that you can inflate by mouth in a few seconds. One of these, weighing only an ounce or so, can be carried readily accessible during cold weather and used, too, as a dry seat.

Using Stuff Bags

Surprisingly small stuff bags are now available in which to cram sleeping bags. This method of packing not only cuts down on bulk; it also saves the sleeping robe from week after week of weakening strap pressure in the same spots, and it helps to keep the filler fluffed up.

Making a Browse Bed

Everyone owes it to himself to spend at least one night deep in the woods on a browse bed. A real browse bed, something to be enjoyed these days only in real wilderness, is not made by lopping off half a dozen evergreen boughs and dropping them beneath the tree where one's sleeping bag is to be spread. A really comfortable browse bed is thatched. Movies accomplish the task in a minute or so, despite such diversions as turning just in time to club an onrushing wolf or other menace. But in real life and without interruptions, the process requires more like half an hour.

As old outdoorsmen sometimes remark, they go into the woods to have a good time, and a third of that time is spent in bed. You won't have an enjoyable or even a refreshing vacation unless you get a reasonably relaxing sleep most nights—and it is in the bed that most of the beginner's discomfort starts. When an experienced woodsman makes a camp, he gives attention to his bed first of all.

He wants it warm, soft, dry, and smooth. He therefore selects a level, clean, dry piece of ground about three feet wide by seven feet long. First pulling up any shrubs, dislodging a stone or two with a heel, and perhaps knocking out a root, he cuts four poles and stakes them in a rectangle. He can then, if he wants, fill this with pine needles or other forest litter and let it go at that. However the best mattress that can be extemporized from forest materials, if you have the time—*and if you are surrounded by such an abundance of growth that the damage will be of no account*—is one built of evergreen boughs.

The springiest evergreen branches obtainable are needed for this. Best, for example, are the small boughs of the heavily needled balsam. All such branches can be most easily carried to the bed if they are dropped one by one over the handle of an ax. The needles will then interlock, holding the entire load in place. If you are using a knife, which will be entirely adequate, a stick with an up-pointing stub will serve just as well.

The way to start making a browse bed is by placing a deep layer of boughs at the head. The branches are laid upside down, opposite to the way they grow. The butts point toward the foot of the bed and are well covered by succeeding layers. Row after row is laid in this manner. The final mattress should be at least one foot thick. It should be leveled off and given additional resiliency by young evergreen tips shoved in wherever a space can be found.

The first night on such a bed is something that everyone should experience at least once. The second night it will be a bit lumpy. After the third night, you will probably bring in a load of fresh boughs and, after fluffing and rearranging the old aromatic bed, renovate it by interposing new materials as effectively as possible.

4/Tent and Tentless Camping

4

Warmth from Your Campfire

There's nothing quite like those overnight camps on backpacking vacations. Along many of the main trails, lean-tos and other shelters are so spaced that difficulties, even in stormy weather, are reduced to a minimum. But the camps you make along some of the wilderness ways, where you can set up your own bivouac, are usually the most unforgettable.

Suppose you have a small fire built in front of your tarpaulin or plastic shelter, which is pitched like a lean-to to circulate the heat over your bed, and the weather turns nippier or downright cold. Unless you have already provided for some other reflecting area, when the evening meal is over, drive a couple of stout posts about ten inches behind the backlog of your present fire, slanting them a little backwards. Pile up a wall of as rugged logs as you can manage, dry or green, against these. Pretty soon you will have quite a blaze, with the log wall in the rear beating the heat across your bed. If you build up this fire just before turning in, you may be able to keep it going all night. It will provide warmth while you sleep, and in the morning a layer of coals for cooking.

There is no sure formula for keeping a campfire alive all night without attention. Sometimes it will hold. But if heat is necessary for comfortable sleeping, the increasing coldness usually awakens you in a few hours. You grope sleepily for the handy woodpile and toss some sticks into the embers. The pieces flare up quickly, and pretty soon you begin to feel the fresh heat.

You stay hunched up on one elbow. There is a wind high in the trees. Some bird you've never heard before calls in the distance. The smoke smells sweet. An owl hoots. It's good to be awake that time of night. You finally lie back and relax. Almost at once, it is morning; after breakfast you're ready to travel again. *Put your fire dead out.*

A Handy Poncho

A fifteen-ounce poncho, 5½ by 7½ feet, which folds into a pocket-sized wad, will keep even the backpacker's knees dry in wet going in the open, and will ward off chilly wind along the ridges. It will also quickly waterproof a makeshift lean-to shelter. On nights when you prefer to sleep beneath the stars, this poncho will protect your sleeping bag from ground damp. (Take a light mosquito bar into country where you may need one.)

A Sheet of Plastic

The simplest form of shelter is merely a large sheet of plastic which, if it is of light material, will fold and stow handily in a breast pocket. These are so convenient to carry, as a matter of fact, that I always have one with me when I go into the woods. With such protection, even in a downpour you can boil the kettle and have lunch while remaining comfortable and dry. It is easy, too, to improvise a sleeping shelter. A plastic sheet quickly waterproofs a pile of equipment, and protects it from the heavy dews often encountered even on fair nights.

Where these plastic tarps are most handy is in forested wilderness. There you can quickly and easily throw up a shelter with boughs, but you may have trouble making it waterproof. Here the plastic can be sandwiched in the roof in between the layers of boughs. Along the main, heavily frequented trails such shelters should never be built except in an emergency, because they involve defacing the trees.

In these areas the plastic can be used to waterproof the roof of a lean-to framed of forest litter. Or it can be pitched as a tent. One way to do this is by stretching it over a rope or pole extended between two trees, then weighing down the back, and also the sides if it's that big, with rocks or other poles. A large one pitched as a canopy really makes cooking and eating a pleasure on a stormy day.

Any plastic sheeting will do. However, reinforced plastic tarps are made especially for this type of packsack camping, with nylon threads woven into them and with well-spaced grommets.

If you want to make a more secure job of pitching the ordinary light rectangle of plastic that has no grommets, instead of just weighing it down, special clamps called *visklamps* are available. The tarp material, which may be any light fabric, as well as plastic, is wrapped around the ball part of the clamp, and both are inserted in a ring section to the open end of which a rope is tied. These are light and inexpensive. Another way to go about this, although it is harder on the material, is to make the tie over a twig or stone inside a fold of the sheeting.

An Inexpensive Tarpaulin

Tarpaulins are generally conveniently large in size, while being light in weight. They are inexpensive and may be used in a number of different ways. The disadvantages on a hiking trip are that they are apt to involve more fabric, and therefore more weight, than a specially cut small tent.

One answer to that problem is the economical shelter tarp shown here, made in any size desired, either of light waterproof fabric or of durable plastic sheeting. This type cuts out a lot of excess material.

Even this small a lean-to bivouac provides comfort and an enjoyable convenience. You profit to the fullest reasonable degree from your fire while you sleep, when it's cold enough to keep a blaze going and when

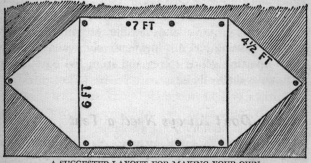

A SUGGESTED LAYOUT FOR MAKING YOUR OWN
SMALL SHELTER TARP.

you are where you can do this. And when you awake in the morning, there is the sky to study for weather hints and the surrounding country to scan.

When you are sitting in front of your small cooking fire preparing your meals, you will have plenty of room for food and utensils on either side. When you lean back to relax after supper, you can enjoy the color and hearty warmth of your fire.

Such a shelter, with triangular wings forming side walls when it is erected, can be easily put up in a few minutes. I usually look for a tree to support one end of the ridgepole and use a couple of poles tied together like shears at the other end. The top of the shelter ties to this ridge.

For the back, it's often handiest to locate a fair-sized pole and stake it in position, then tie the lower part of the rear wall to this instead of bothering with stakes. Not only is this practice generally faster and easier, but it makes a more substantial job that keeps out furtive drafts. In really cold weather, when you can do it, imitate the trapper and choose a cubbyhole for your camp site—a sheltered spot among thickly spreading spruce, or perhaps a tiny clearing in a thick fir grove.

Incidentally, both the necessary grommets and grommet-setting kits are inexpensively available from many sporting goods stores and from the equipment companies that sell fabrics.

You Don't Always Need a Tent

The preceding illustrates some of the possibilities. In other words, you don't necessarily need a tent. This is especially true along the great trails where frequent

free shelters await the hiker—although on the more
popular stretches one may come to such a way station
and find campers already relaxing in it.

Tentless camping, particularly if you include some
provision for emergency shelter in your outfit, is also
practical in other areas. And no wilderness nights
are more memorable, in good weather, than those
spent entirely in the open.

Wilderness Bivouacking

Often you may be out when the night is cold, or at
least cool; and there may be rain, or even snow. A
blazing campfire will be needed just as soon as you
can get one going. You will still need shelter of some
sort, though.

In the true wilderness forests of this country, away
from the most heavily traveled hiking trails, this is no
problem. Even a big tree with thick foliage will ward
off a lot of weather. One of the easiest and best overnight niches can be quickly made, as a matter of fact,
by stripping off enough lower branches from a short,
thick evergreen to form a small cubbyhole. These
branches, supplemented with more from other trees,
can be used to make a soft, dry flooring and to thatch
the roof and sides.

An evergreen bivouac of this sort is so easily and
rapidly fashioned that in deep wilderness—in chilly
weather—I have often made them so as to enjoy
more fully the noon tea pail and lunch. The tree
chosen should first be shaken free of any snow or
rain. If a storm has settled in heavily, a few pieces of
birch bark or similar forest material will shed a lot of
moisture.

If the dusk that is dropping quickly over the forest is bringing a deepening cold, try to select your site in a thick clump of small trees. If possible, let it be half-way down the lee slope of a hill, as this is the warmest spot in most country.

During the daylight that is left, haul in all the dry, dead firewood you can find in the immediate locality. You may need a lot to last out the night. Include a few damp or rotting stumps and snags if possible, and perhaps a recently fallen big green limb or so, as these will be handy for holding a more even heat and retaining the fire.

If time is pressing, kindle your fire at nightfall and complete your preparations by its illumination. Make everything as ready and comfortable as you reasonably can. If your clothes are damp, get them dry before trying to sleep. This you will probably be able to accomplish faster if you take most of them off and stretch and hang them not too close to flames and sparks.

Then put the heaviest and longest-lasting wood on the fire, arranging it so that the blaze will be a little longer than your body. Stretch out, relax, and let the hoo-ho-ho-hooing of owls, the yipping of coyotes, or a chorus of timber wolves lull you to sleep.

In several hours or so, the coldness will invariably awaken you. The fire has burned to embers. You grope for the woodpile and toss some sticks into the coals. The pieces flare up quickly, and you soon feel the warm again. This may happen several times, but it is more pleasant than disagreeable.

Siwashing When It's Colder

It is not enough in colder weather for the hiker merely to build a fire and stretch out beside it. Unless other provisions are made, such a blaze would warm you only in front; those parts of your body facing away from it would be so uncomfortably cold that restorative sleep would be impossible. Under such conditions you need to consider ways of confining and reflecting the heat and keeping the frosty breezes away.

One very easy solution is to arrange some sort of a ridge pole about four feet off the ground, perhaps laying it between rocks or trees. Lean poles or sticks against this at such an angle that they will reach the ground along the long back edge of your bed. Make your fire so that it will warm the entire length of your body.

On these poles, shingle or lay a quantity of spruce boughs, leafy branches, bark, or the like. You can even lean small evergreen trees in place without any bracing poles, hooking alternate ones across the ridge so as to present a thick, uniform wall against the night. The result in either case will be an open-faced camp with the fire built along the front. Shingle in the ends of your lean-to also, or pile a few small evergreens there too.

If you can kindle your fire against some reflecting surface, so much the better. The snugger you make your camp and the better the firewood you haul in, the longer your naps will be. There is no sense in being cold in a wooded country. It's true that under favorable conditions nothing is more enjoyable than just spreading your sleeping bag on the pine needles. There are other nights, however, when a half hour occupied in readying a bivouac will be essential to convenience, well-being, and over-all enjoyment of the experience.

There are no set rules governing siwashing while backpacking. You do the best you can, as quickly as you can, with the materials at hand. A shallow cave may be at hand where, warmed by a fire in front, you can rest as cozily as our earliest ancestors did in such a place.

Two or three boulders may be so grouped that when a bough roof is thrown over them, they will afford snug sanctuary. A crude triangle stamped in the snow, with the larger end floored and roofed with evergreen boughs and with a small fire in the remaining corner, will provide warmth and shelter if one is caught by a mountain storm and has inadequate equipment. The main thing in such circumstances is to keep everything dry, as clothing and other essentials which become damp or frozen lose the quality of insulation.

Carrying Plastic Tubing

The cheapest, and in many ways the handiest, tentage to lug along on the main hiking trails is just a section of large plastic tubing. Such plastic tubes are available from sporting goods stores and outfitters. There is one made of polyethylene which is nine feet seven inches long and has a circumference of eight feet. The simplest way to erect it is by running a rope through the tube to serve as a ridge and tying

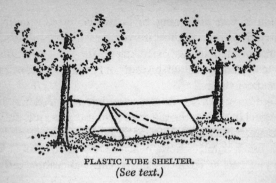

PLASTIC TUBE SHELTER.
(See text.)

this several feet high between two trees. No pegs are necessary. The weight of the occupant anchors the tent.

This particular tube weighs one pound and costs about two and a half dollars, making it practical for short trips with the family where a number of inexpensive shelters may be needed. Such tubing can also be obtained in longer lengths, so that you can sleep one individual at each open end if you wish.

The tubing utilized by dry cleaners can also be pressed into service, but this is excessively fragile. Even the tubing mentioned above, although more durable than that used by dry cleaners, is very vulnerable. Particular care should be taken with the underneath portions, as they puncture easily.

The Comfortable Forester Tent

One of the pleasantest parts of any hiking vacation should be the camps. For these—especially if you want to build your own tent and at the same time cut weight and costs—the Forester Tent is a good solution if you are going to be traveling in wooded country. It is one of the best tents ever devised for a chronic outdoorsman, particularly for one who objects to spending any of his outdoor hours confined in a closed canvas cell.

The Forester Tent is the cheapest of all tents, in ratio to size and convenience, to make yourself. It is the easiest and quickest to pitch. Considering its weight and bulk, it is the most comfortable in which to live and do your few camp chores. With the exception of some of the special lean-to tents such as the Whelen, it is the easiest to warm with a campfire out front.

The one weak point of the Forester—at first glance, anyway—is that if you try to mosquitoproof it, you ruin its inexpensiveness and functional simplicity. But in bug time it is an easy matter to secure a light mosquito bar for a dollar or two and hang or stake this net enclosure over your bed.

The Forester Tent is triangular in shape. The tent can be built in any size of course. But the smallest really comfortable dimensions for one backpacker, or for two who do not mind a bit of crowding, are about seven feet wide at the open front, three feet at the back, and seven feet deep from front to rear. The peak of such a model should stand about six feet above the ground in front, while the triangular rear will be about three feet high. With the entire tent open to the fire in front, the angle will be such that heat and light will be reflected throughout the sheltered area.

The tent is usually pitched with three poles and eight sticks procured at the campsite. The ridge pole should be long enough to extend from the peak and to pass down and out through the hole at the top of the back wall at such a tilt that it will rest on the ground about three feet behind the tent. The two shorter poles are arranged at the front like shears and, holding the ridge pole at their apex, run from the front corners to the peak.

You pitch this tent with its back to the prevailing wind. But if the wind shifts around to the front, and brings rain or snow with it, the front of the tent and the more exposed parts of the bedding can get wet. This is why some makers sew a hood or flap to the front of the shelter that can be stretched out protectively in case of storm. A poncho or any small piece of canvas or plastic can also be used to close the top of the open space.

In any event, the entire front should not be closed all the way to the ground. If only the top part is shut, or if in ordinary cases a flap is extended outward, moisture will be kept out. It will be possible, at the same time, to cook comfortably during a storm. Another advantage inherent with this particular type of tent is that one is so easy to handle that only a very few minutes will be required to strike and then erect it again with its back to the new wind direction. Made in this small size, of one of the light waterproof tent fabrics, such a tent need not weigh more than three pounds or so.

The pattern for making a Forester Tent, passed along to me by Colonel Townsend Whelen, is shown here. Colonel Whelen's directions were: "This tent is for one or two campers, with beds arranged along the side walls. Cut and sew to the dimensions shown, allowing one inch all around the edges for hemming.

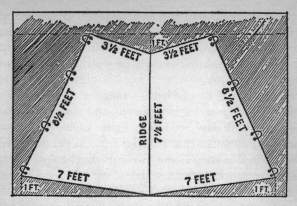

SUGGESTED PATTERN FOR MAKING YOUR OWN FORESTER TENT.
(See text.)

"Note how the bottom of the sides is set back one foot to make the tent sit right on the ground. To manage this, cut the pattern from rectangular fabric as shown, then angle the front and back. The rear wall—an isosceles triangle three feet high, with a three-foot base and three-and-one-half-foot sides, not including the one-inch allowance for hemming—is cut off square at the top. When this portion is sewed to the main body of the tent at the rear, it leaves a hole at the top of the rear through which the ridge pole is stuck. It makes about the most comfortable camp imaginable."

Types of Store Tents

The choice of a tent is so very much an individual matter that there are many models provided from which to choose. All backpacking tents, however, have to have two characteristics in common. They have to be light and compact to carry. Beyond that, what you select will depend on personal preference, the amount you want to pay, the kind of country to be traversed, and the amount of weight you want to allocate to shelter.

There is plenty of choice—ranging from crawl-in tents weighing about two pounds and costing around twenty-five dollars to small, light, somewhat more spacious one-man tents weighing closer to three pounds and costing about twice as much. When two vacationists are hiking together, they can get a larger tent, big enough for both, and divide the weight (although not necessarily the tenting equipment) between them.

This ratio of weight per hiker continues in the trail models of the larger tents. Some big enough to sleep four, complete with pole assemblies for use in the mountains above the timber line, weigh only twelve pounds, which is three pounds per camper. Prices among the big specialists in such equipment run from about $60 to $135, to give you an idea.

Store Poles and Pegs

Poles can save time, especially with some models of tents. The main determining factor is where you'll be doing your hiking. In forested country, it's usually no problem to get your height with cords suspended from rocks or trees. This is not always possible in the desert or in the high mountains above the timber line.

Except in extreme country, though, pegs are something else again. You can cut them where there is forest growth. In the woods, as a matter of fact, it is often preferable to lay poles into position and guy the bottom of the tent to these. If there are no trees, one can use a few rocks. The main thing to be said in favor of store pegs is that they save time. But ordinarily you've plenty of time, and you can stay out longer and more comfortably if you convert those extra ounces into food.

Water Repellents and Waterproofing

The problem isn't getting a waterproof fabric. This you can achieve by coating the material. This is all right if the tent is to be open, like the campfire models. But if the area is to be largely closed—perhaps against dampness, which is the only reason for waterproofing in the first place—the moisture being given off continuously by the body will condense on cold sides of the tent and wet the occupants. It will generally be sort of like living in a steam bath.

The trouble with water repellents that let the fabrics breathe is of course that they are just that— repellents only. With the small type of tent that is used on backpacking expeditions, it becomes almost impossible not to start leaks by rubbing against the walls, which at best do not have the steep sides necessary to run off moisture effectively.

One answer to this is waterproofing the lower parts of the walls, which eiderdowns, and inhabitants can scarcely avoid touching. This, along with a waterproof floor, works out well enough in ordinary cases. And it helps to keep a tent dry when it's pitched in snow.

But how about when rain causes you to hole up for several days? The best answer is a separate fly. Pitched only when needed, this can be entirely waterproof, as there will be enough space between it and the tent to permit adequate ventilation. The fly can be of extremely light material, to cut down weight. As far as that goes, the fly need cover only the really vulnerable portions of the shelter, where leakage is most likely and where such leakage will cause problems.

This sort of fly is particularly advantageous when made of nylon, at once the lightest and strongest tent material—but one that is not at its best in wet weather. A tightly woven cotton, taking and holding the numerous kinds of water repellents and doing so efficiently, would be a far better bet in stormy weather if it were not for these two exceptional characteristics of nylon. As it is, you can use a light nylon tent and fly and still be ahead of the game.

Most Popular Fabrics

Cotton is still the old camping standby. A good tightly woven cotton fabric weighing some five ounces per square yard will turn away water about as well as a coated nylon if the tent is well made and is put up without too many wrinkles, if the pitch is steep, and if the tent is large enough so that the inside walls can be kept clear. However, the special lightweight requirements of backpacking tents generally nullify these last two requirements.

Cotton has another disadvantage when it comes to backpacking. The world is unusually inviting after a night storm, say, and beckons the hiker to pack his gear and hit the trail early. But cotton, especially when rolled up while damp, is very prone to mildew and rot. Incidentally, this one characteristic by itself makes all cotton tents and tarpaulins very much of an all-time problem where the climate is hot and humid.

Considerable experimentation is still going on with nylon tent fabrics, still the lightest, strongest, and toughest available. One fairly recent answer has been DuPont Nylon Type 330, developed by DuPont in co-operation with Burlington Industrial Fabrics Company and now widely available both in actual tents and in fabrics for those who would make their own.

Weighing only four and a quarter ounces per square yard, this new breathable material nevertheless has strength to spare; and a new weaving and finishing technique eliminates the absolute need for coating. Condensation has been reduced to what is generally a satisfactory degree. The fabric also shows superior resistance to deterioration usually associated with storage and to extended exposure to sunlight as well. However, it does still leave something to be desired in heavy downpours, and experiments go on.

For any up-to-the-moment developments in the fabric field, write the following weavers:

Burlington Industries, Inc.
1345 Avenue of Americas
New York, N.Y. 10019

Stern & Stern Textile, Inc.
Hornell, N.Y. 14843

J. P. Stevens & Co., Inc.
1185 Avenue of Americas
New York, N.Y. 10036

5/What About Your Clothing?

5

Comfortable Foot Travel

The boot, where the hiker and the trail meet, is the most important part of the clothing category. Poorly fitted and chosen footwear has taken the edge off far too many hiking vacations. The vacationist taking to the trails for the first time, on a trip that requires long and difficult foot travel, is apt to discover when it's too late that he is committed to footwear that will handicap or badly cripple him. Thus the grand outing he has been planning, maybe for years, is ruined.

The shoe size you wear in the city—and the one the average salesman there will measure you for—will perhaps do well enough for the several miles of walking which many individuals cover on a usual outing. But beware of this size for a daily tramp of eight to twenty miles over wild country, especially if it is hilly country.

One such excursion in city-sized footwear will almost certainly lay you up with blisters and abrasions. After three or four miles of hiking over rugged terrain, your feet swell considerably because of the repeated and varying pressures of walking and because of the increased blood supply that is being pumped

into them by the stimulation of exercise. The shoes
you select must be large enough to remain comfortable when your feet are in this enlarged condition.

Selecting the Right Socks

The simple but all-important formula for wilderness
walking is heavy socks and big shoes. Regardless of
heat or cold, dryness or dampness, only wool socks
are suitable for long hikes—although you may like
nylon reinforcements at the toes and heels to extend
their lives.

These socks may vary from thin to medium during
the summer, and from medium to heavy during the
frosty months. Throughout the year, however, you
want only top-quality, finely processed, and well-
made woolens. Don't have anything to do with
shoddy ones if you can possibly avoid it. Poor woolens
mat. They contain impurities that irritate the feet.
They wear poorly. As for loosely and skimpily knit
socks, these are an abomination from the first day
you put them on.

A few individuals' feet seem to be allergic to wool.
Such hikers can often wear thin socks of some other
material under the wool. These may be made of
cotton. Some select nylon, which is certainly long-
wearing but is, for many of us, a lot too slippery unless worn too tightly or gartered in some manner,
neither of which is compatible with the outdoor
routine.

Taking the thickness of your socks into consideration, here is a general rule you can apply in selecting
the ideal size of footwear for hard outdoor wear.
With one pair of thin or medium wool socks, have

your shoes one full size longer and one full size wider than your proper fit in city shoes. For heavy socks, have them one and one-half sizes longer and wider. If half sizes are not available, increase to the next full size.

For the additional pair of socks that may be desirable in extremely cold weather, experiment to get the same comparative freedom of fit as above. Incidentally, three closely packed pairs of socks afford less warmth than do two loose pairs. Aside from the fact that circulation is impeded by such a tight fit, the resulting compression of the fibers cuts down on the insulative dead-air space.

There is an entirely different way to combat cold feet, inasmuch as limits of effective insulation on the feet are rather quickly reached. This is one reason that the answer to cold feet isn't necessarily thicker and warmer footwear. Oddly enough, it is an extra shirt or some other additional insulation around the waist, chest, and back that may warm the feet, without any alteration of footwear.

Depending on the requirements, the body is always regulating its heat, either warming or cooling itself. An accumulation of excess heat in the torso results in a cooling requirement. This is achieved by directing the overwarm blood to the extremities, which act as radiators. The effect can be concentrated in the feet by keeping the head and hands extra warm.

Adding Insoles for Support

Insoles are frequently added to provide additional insulation, cushioning, arch support, and a more comfortable fit. They are most frequently made of leather, felt, or lambskin, all of which pick up moisture and should be taken out periodically for drying separately.

Insoles are also obtainable in woven synthetic fiber, non-absorbent and non-matting, the loose structure of which helps ventilate the feet.

Breaking In Footwear

It is highly important that you break in new footwear well in advance of a trip. Some of us have feet that are shaped differently from normal, probably because of improper fittings in city shoes. The lasts on which good outdoor shoes are made, changing as foot sizes themselves have changed over the generations, are designed for normal proportions.

When shoes are new, even when correctly fitted, they may bring undue pressure on parts of your feet. The new footwear will gradually stretch at those points, however, if broken in slowly and easily.

There are two functional ways of breaking in new leather shoes. You can do it gradually by hiking two miles the first day, three miles the second, and so on up to five miles—by which time the process should be completed. The second method consists of standing in four inches of water for fifteen minutes and then hiking until the shoes dry on your feet.

Hiking in High-Top Boots

High tops almost always sag and wrinkle more or less at the ankles. This can bring pressure on the Achilles tendon at the back of your ankle. It is true that this becomes negligible in the case of gradually softened and sufficiently broken-in leather tops, and that in any boot it can be offset to a large extent by the insertion of some stiffener—such as a folded heavy paper or a piece of birch bark.

If the pressure is not relieved, it will set up a painful inflammation of the sheath through which this greatest tendon of our body runs. Medically this is known as *synovitis*. The only cure for this is ten days off the feet.

There is also the weight factor. A boot with a ten-inch top will weigh about eight ounces more than one which is six inches high. This is an additional half-pound to be lifted three inches high and to be carried twenty-eight inches ahead about 2,500 times every mile! Such additional expenditure of energy really accumulates and is felt on a long, all-day tramp.

Hiking in Canvas Sneakers

Ordinary rubber-soled sneakers and basketball shoes are popular along fairly smooth wilderness ways, such as the Appalachian Trail, and in comparatively dry country such as that found along stretches of the Sierra Trail. For rugged use don't buy the low ones, however. Select those with tops about six inches high. The rubber soles should be roughly corrugated or substantially cleated as a safeguard against slipping.

The chief advantage afforded by such footwear is that of lightness, which is a joy. Although such shoes do not hold up long, they offer an inexpensive way to outfit the growing children in a family. They are best worn with one pair of medium-weight woolen socks. They are not very durable. A hundred miles over rough terrain is about the limit for most. But they are comparatively cheap.

Sneakers soon wet through in rain, even in the morning dew. But this makes no particular difference, for they dry out quickly and without becoming stiff.

Rubber Bottoms and Leather Tops

Boots with leather tops and rubber bottoms are popular on such trails as the Appalachian and Vermont's Long Trail when it's wet under foot in the spring and fall. For practically all wear, unless there is a definite reason to the contrary, they should be purchased with tops only six or eight inches high.

These boots should be worn with one or two pairs of wool socks and with insoles. For those who do not care for the flatfooted sensation that is characteristic of most such rubbers, leather insoles with arch supports are available. For very cold weather these may be obtained with clipped lambskin next to the feet.

The better boots of this sort are also ideal for deer and other big-game hunting in the fall, except in the steepest country, because they are almost noiseless and can be kept water repellent clear to the top.

They're not good for wear in the very steep mountains of the West, particularly not on abrupt snow-covered slopes. However, they can be very comfortably used in winter down to about twenty degrees below zero; they get pretty frosty much below that range. If they are worn with adequate insoles and not laced too tightly, the insoles and socks compress with each step and pump air in and out, ventilating the feet and making these boots excellent for summers where even in fair weather the ground is often wet with dew and where there are swamplands.

Regular Hiking Boots

The proven favorites among most trail veterans, especially in the West, are the special boots—both imported and domestic—stocked by the big catalogue-issuing sporting goods dealers for the express purpose of hiking. Equipped with the best of rubber lug soles, these afford high traction and long wear. They are safe, comfortable, and quiet, but not inexpensive. With reasonable care they are good for years, especially as they can be resoled when necessary.

If your sporting goods dealer cannot readily obtain these for you locally, it is practical to order them by mail, as a proper fit is guaranteed. To measure your feet, put on the socks you intend to wear on the trail. Then stand on a piece of paper, distributing your weight equally on both feet. Holding a pencil vertically, clearly make the outline of each foot. Send these outlines to the outfitter, along with a notation of the length and width of your normal dress shoes.

Cleated Rubber Soles

Neoprene cleated rubber soles are available that will grip on almost everything except glare ice and ice-covered rock. These soles are the same type found on many of the best trail boots. Not only do they make resoling of regular mountain boots possible, but they can also be attached to other shoes.

This makes it possible to turn a favorite pair of

leather work or hunting boots into good trail performers, at the same time saving money. It is not practical, however, to buy such boots for this purpose, because for very little more money you can purchase ready-made boots especially designed for trail work.

These soles are generally available in two treads. One of these types of soles (of which there are different makes) has a deeper cleat, for longer and more useful life during general hiking. A lighter model has shallower cleats designed more particularly for rock climbing.

Cleating with Hobnails

Hobnails, although noisy and requiring skillful use on smooth rock, still have their advocates. They are better than rubber on ice, crusted snow, and wet mossy slants. Hobnails can be applied to any of the birdshooter or army marching shoes, provided these have leather soles. Nails and calks will not, of course, stick in either composition or rubber bottoms.

Available from the big sporting goods outfitters, hobnails can be installed locally if you wish. The square edging nails are placed about an inch apart around the edge of the sole and heel—insuring against front, back, and side slipping on any surface except hard, smooth rock. They should be cleated all the way through the edge of the sole outside of the uppers.

The round interior nails may be ordinary cone-shaped hobnails, which are procurable anywhere. They prevent slipping to some extent. Their principal function, however, is to keep the inside of the sole from wearing too fast. They should be cleated through the outer leather sole only, never through the inner sole, or they will eventually dig into your feet. Doing it this way means an extra job for the shoemaker. Regardless of this, make certain that he does not cleat through the upper sole.

Relaxing in Moccasins

You'll want a light pair of footwear into which to change when you make camp. Many hikers choose moccasins for this purpose. Most satisfactory in many respects are those with substantial, deeply cut rubber or composition soles that can be used for some hiking if necessary.

Best Treatment of Leather

Wet leather footwear can be very quickly ruined if dried out near a campfire or shelter stove. The best treatment is to scrape and wash off any dirt and mud, wipe off any free moisture, and then allow the gear to dry slowly in the air. If the bottoms are leather, the shape will be better retained if the boots are first straightened and then stuffed with something such as paper, dry clothes, or moss.

If any artificial warmth at all is used, it should be extremely mild. Even the procedure of hanging footwear at the far end of a hot cabin can very easily stiffen, shrink, crack, and ruin the leather. It is often best to be philosophical at the end of the day about wet shoes—figuring that if the trail is wet, they'll soon be soaked again anyway.

After boots are nearly dry (and periodically, as at supply points), they should be rubbed with Neatsfoot oil or any good boot conditioner. These will go on easier and penetrate better if the leather is slightly warm. They should be rubbed with particular energy into wrinkles, stitchings, and the partition between the upper part and the sole.

Leather footwear cannot be made entirely waterproof; nor would this be desirable. It would defeat its own purpose, by trapping perspiration and soon making the feet more uncomfortably wet than would be the case under ordinary conditions with leather that could breathe.

Boots may be fairly waterproof when new. After a few miles of hiking they will leak more or less at the seams, and during continued immersion some water will work through the leather. If dubbing is then worked thoroughly into the seams, they will again be fairly waterproof for a little while until the preparation wears off. This is one reason why leather footwear should be well treated about once a week when in use. Treating it too often, of course, can make it too soft.

When boots are to be put away until the next season, scrape all dirt or mud from them with a flat stick or brush. Wash with a mild soap and very little water, using a small handbrush. Remove all suds and wipe the insides dry with a clean cloth. It is a good idea to keep them in shape either by inserting boot trees or by stuffing them with crumpled newspapers. Then grease and store them, away from pests, in a reasonably cool and dry place.

Taking Care of the Feet

Wear only well-fitting and fairly new socks, with no rough seams or unduly harsh darned spots. If your feet are tender, dust both them and your socks the first week with foot powder. Giving them alcohol baths at supply points will help toughen them.

In any event, wash your feet at least every night and change your socks daily. When the going is rough, it is refreshing to stop when possible during the day and bathe the feet. A lot of us carry an extra pair of socks on the outside of the pack to switch to at that time. Actually, when the way is hot and you're perspiring considerably, the thing to do is to change socks frequently, hanging the damp socks on the outside of the pack where they can dry.

Good woolen socks are easily washed without shrinking, with soap and barely warm water. They should be rinsed, gently squeezed reasonably free of moisture without wringing, and stretched back into shape to dry slowly—preferably in the open breeze, but in any event well back from the campfire.

Choosing Appropriate Clothing

This varies depending on the climate, and you need to make inquiries about what is most often worn where you plan to hike. One thing always holds true though: You should wear comfortable undergarments that will not bind or chafe. Cotton is a common choice.

Generally speaking an individual doing the relatively hard work of hiking perspires freely, and his clothing becomes more or less wet. Cotton garments

are best for all hot and warm climates, because they
are coolest. The perspiration which they absorb, however, makes them so cold that they can chill one as
soon as this function slows down. When cotton is worn,
the hiker should preferably have a rubdown and
change to dry clothing as soon as he gets to camp. At
least, if he is at all chilly, he should put on a woolen
shirt or some other warm garment when he stops for
the night.

For a cold or even merely chilly climate, all but the
underclothing should be light wool throughout. Wool
also gets wet from perspiration, but much of the
water passes through it to be evaporated on the outside. And wet wool does not feel particularly cold. It
does not chill like wet cotton, except when the wind
is blowing very strongly. Under these circumstances,
common on the high trails, a closely woven but still
porous outside jacket of thin cotton should be taken
to be slipped on as a windbreak.

Wool is warm chiefly because of the insulating effect of the dead air held in the numerous tiny spaces
among its fibers. A pair of light wool garments are
warmer than a heavy one of the same total weight
because of the additional air contained between the
two of them.

In extremely cold weather one can freeze quickly
in wet clothing. It is very necessary under such circumstances to keep from perspiring excessively. This
you can easily accomplish by shedding layers of
clothing as you warm up, thereby always remaining
moderately cool.

In fact, the layer system is always best on the trail.
In the chill of the morning, whether on the quickly
varying desert or high on a northern range, many

like to start with everything on. But I, for one, find it easier to get along if I start cold and get up warmth by walking. In either case, you shed layers as the sun climbs higher.

There is one thing to watch out for though: that is, not to carry this too far. In the thin, dry air of upper altitudes the sun burns deeply, even through a basic low-country tan. Back and shoulders are especially vulnerable.

It is always best to anticipate heat changes whenever possible—to open the clothing before you actually start to perspire, and to close it again before really feeling chilly. This takes a certain amount of experience, and is often one of the signs that a beginner is maturing into a veteran.

Shorts, if you like them, are fine on many trails, particularly those that are not too bushy. But it is always a mistake to wear them all day, and take a chance of crippling yourself by sunburn, until your skin has toughened.

Be sure that clothing is not too tight or restrictive. Knees in particular should work freely. Many like to have dirt-collecting cuffs removed and trousers stagged about three inches shorter than city trousers. Otherwise the trousers' legs have the habit of catching on snags and tripping one.

Picking out clothing with fast, bright colors has several virtues. You are less likely to strike camp and leave some article behind drying on a bush. There is the factor of safety if you travel during hunting seasons, which for some game or other may last the year around. Such a selection can also do a lot for color photography.

The Eiderdown Jacket

A light eiderdown jacket is one of the most comfortable garments I know of to put on when you stop, tired and enthusiastic, for the night. These are even handy on the desert, as most desert country gets surprisingly cold as soon as the sun sinks. And the heat, with little moisture in the atmosphere to beat it back, goes out of the sand and rocks.

At night when you sit in front of your campfire, one feels luxurious against your otherwise chilly back. If your sleeping bag is the least bit cold when you go to bed, spread this jacket between the robe and the mattress.

Pockets in Your Clothing

Although most belongings can be carried more comfortably in the packsack, pockets are still handy on a hiking trip; so special attention should be paid to their deepness and ruggedness when you buy clothing for a trip. Because of the danger of losing your already limited essentials it is well to get most or all of these with fasteners. Even on the side trouser pockets, slide fasteners are often available; or you can install them yourself, using an especially smooth and husky zipper.

No compromise should be made with shirt pockets. Flap closures, buttoned or otherwise secured, are best. But if you have an old shirt that you plan to wear out on a trip and it has open pockets, install flaps or at the very least snaps. With the latter arrangement, you'll have to secure the contents further

—as with a handkerchief wadded across the top of the opening.

The side trouser pockets should not be loaded (as is often done) in such a way that they interfere with free leg motion. As for pockets low on the legs, the feature of some older military surplus clothing, experiments have shown that it is three times more tiring to carry anything here than on the back.

Rainwear, Kerchiefs, and Windbreakers

The poncho mentioned in Chapter Four is best for foul-weather wear. It is useful for ground-sheet, shelter, and other trail functions. When it is worn during rain, it is loose enough to permit ventilation. This looseness can be a problem on a windy day, but it is far preferable to encasing the body in closely fitting rainwear that would soon have you wet with perspiration.

One or two large bandana kerchiefs are always coming in handy. In really hot going, some hikers carry one in the belt to wipe off accumulating perspiration. Some twist one around the forehead to keep perspiration out of the eyes. In cold weather the bandana can be worn around one's neck as a barrier against rising body warmth. They can also be used where needed as pads or to ease chafing. In an emergency they can serve as triangular bandages or a sling. They also afford a certain amount of wind, sun, and insect protection.

Loose layers of clothing give the most efficient insulation for their weight. But the air currents set up by body motion, and those from the outside, can take away most of this insulative value by preventing the establishment of dead air. Something must be provided to keep cooler air from constantly replacing this insulation of inert air. The best way to accomplish this is by donning a windbreaker. This should be as thin as durability will permit. The fabric, often poplin or something similar, should be woven as tightly as possible while still permitting the necessary dissipation of body vapor.

Comfort in a Cold Country

No matter where you go, you'll do well to take the best of outdoor clothing, bought specifically for where you're going. The neatest trick I know of for cold-country comfort lies in some of the insulative underwears.

You have to be careful what you buy, however. Garments made from some of the synthetics trap perspiration as tightly as rubber. In weather that is at all warm, you might as well be traveling in a portable steam bath. In really cold going, more than just discomfort is at stake. Some entrapped perspiration freezes; and if you keep on trying to bull it through, so may you.

The difficulty at the subzero temperatures encountered on some winter trails in the high country is not so much keeping warm, but doing so without too much weight and constraint while maintaining body ventilation. One garment which does this job is an undersuit made with six-once dacron polyester fiberfill insulation quilted inside a 70-denier nylon shell and lining. The considerably more expensive eiderdown, being lighter and more compressible, is even better.

Like eiderdown, this crimped dacron seems to have a built-in thermostat that adjusts it to widely varying temperatures. The easiest way to give this an assist in ordinary cold going is just unzip the garment—as much and for as long as comfortable. I find this satisfactory in temperatures ranging from fifty degrees below zero up to about zero. When the weather becomes balmier, this particular undersuit becomes too warm. Weighing less than two pounds, this is regarded as a heavy suit. Lighter combinations are available for milder climates.

When you are on the trail and the weather gets too warm, just take off either or both of the two parts and stow them in your pack. Together they're far lighter and more compact than one ordinary heavy sweater.

During winter in high country, winds have to be combatted in addition to cold temperatures. In a twenty-mile-an-hour, head-on wind, regular woolen clothing loses about 55 per cent of the warmth it maintains in still air. Get a much faster wind in weather thirty degrees below and, unless you put on windproofs, you feel as if you're wearing burlap. This dacron-insulated nylon checks the wind more effectively than most other satisfactory fabrics not built especially for this purpose. But to get the fullest benefit from such an undersuit, you still need a windbreaker.

A fringe benefit is that such a suit can effectively be worn cold nights as a second sleeping bag inside the regular combination.

6/Packing Up to Go

The Equipment Story
Including Your Compass
Including Dry Matches
Adhesive Bandages and Tape
An Inexpensive Watch
Extra Pair of Glasses
A Magnifying Glass
Some Kind of Mirror
Maps of the Territory
Some Writing Materials
The Books You Want
Things in the Toilet Kit
Binoculars and Camera
Some Lightweight Cord
A Good Insect Repellent
Your Snakebite Kit
—and others

6

The Equipment Story

The maximum weight recommended, even for vigorous and athletic young men, for the first year or two of hiking over the fairly rough and frequently steep trails encountered in wilderness terrain is thirty-five pounds. For young women in comparable top condition the suggested maximum is twenty-five pounds. This is for hikes of two or more days, averaging from five to fifteen miles a day in fairly good weather. It has no connection with the loads that can be packed a few miles to a more or less permanent camp or wrestled a mile or so across a canoe portage.

The tendency at first is to overload, under the impression that a lot of odds and ends are needed to avoid hardships. It is soon discovered, though, that if you take the right articles and use them in the most advantageous ways, there are no hardships.

"It is some advantage to lead a primitive life if only to learn what are the necessaries," an inveterate hiker by the name of Henry Thoreau said over a century ago. "Most of the luxuries and many of the so-called comforts are not only dispensable but positive hindrances."

The pleasure to be derived from any trip into the farther places may be divided into three parts: the zest of getting ready, the journey itself, and the enjoyment of remembering.

For many hikers, preparation is by no means the least of these—the anticipation, the planning, the excitement of thumbing through books and catalogues, and the pleasure of browsing through sporting goods stores.

As each of us looks at the world from a different vantage point, it is only natural that points of view will vary on lesser—and in some instances even on major—items to be included in a backpacking outfit. But as Colonel Townsend Whelen used to say, "I do not, for a minute, suppose my ways are the best ways, but at least it may be helpful to know the other fellow's points."

Including Your Compass

Your compass need not be either large or expensive. Choose one, however, in which the north-pointing end of the needle is unmistakably marked, perhaps by being shaped like an arrow. Some varieties simply have one end of the pointer white and the other black. When someone is mixed up, he often can't remember which is which, particularly as some imports I've seen reverse the usual procedure of letting the more prominent end indicate north. You may prefer a compass on which the entire dial moves.

Compasses are inexpensive. You may as well get a good one, although there is no need (nor is it advisable) to burden yourself with one of the elaborate devices designed more for military use or for surveying. Get a good, small compass that is rugged and preferably waterproof. Keep it where it is handy but where you'll be sure not to lose it. It's not a bad idea to carry a tiny spare in the outfit in real wilderness. There seems to be no good reason to buy a compass that does not have a luminous indicator.

Including Dry Matches

You will want a waterproof container filled with wooden matches on your person whenever you are in the wilderness. The container should be unbreakable, so that even if you should happen to slip in a stream, the matches will remain intact. This match case—which may well include some provision whereby it can be attached to the clothing—should be stowed where it will not be lost.

The wooden matches are best for lighting a fire outdoors anywhere, but on an extended hike their bulk and weight soon add up. Under reasonable conditions, therefore, you will generally be able to leave the emergency supply untouched if you bring along a small supply of paper matches, enough so you can have a book ready for use in a pocket at all times. Such supplies can easily be replenished at outfitting points of course.

Adhesive Bandages and Tape

The little gauze pads centered on short strips of adhesive tape are useful in such a variety of ways that you always seem to be finding a new use for them along the trail if a few are kept in your pockets. Although the original container should be discarded, the adhesive bandages themselves should be left in the sterile wrappings in which most arrive—especially because these coverings also prevent dust and lint from robbing the tape of its sticking power.

Plain bandages are rated best. Those treated with Mercurochrome and other medicaments have no properties that make them superior to ordinary pads, according to most doctors and laboratories. These sources contend that such medication may even be detrimental. Plastic tape is an improvement over fabric, adapting itself more easily and often more substantially to various surfaces.

Prompt use of an inexpensive adhesive bandage the moment part of the foot begins to feel tender will many times prevent formation of a blister, and the subsequent danger of infection. Air will reach the affected part if the bandage is properly applied; so the dressing may be left on while the skin toughens.

Adhesive bandages will also prove convenient for various other uses in the bush—such as repairing binoculars, fishing gear, and even clothing. Adhesive tape is even better for repairing things.

The usual outer covering of adhesive tape should be laid aside before you add the roll to your pack. This tape, when you can get at it handily enough, affords better protection than the bandages for tender spots on the feet. It can be pressed and left over actual blisters as well.

However, tape should never be applied when there are breaks in the skin, as this might easily set up an infection. The often recommended practice of puncturing a blister, by the way, is a poor one in the wilderness because of the danger of infection entering through the break.

An Inexpensive Watch

You can't forget time, even in the wilderness, partly because of the fact that distances back of beyond are so often measured by the time it takes to cover them. And a timepiece can be used under proper conditions to tell direction, based on the fact that at noon sun time the sun is almost due south. Expensive watches should be left at home in most cases, and an inexpensive one bought for the bush.

Extra Pair of Glasses

Anyone who needs glasses will be sensible to carry an extra pair. Along most of the main trails, especially in the mountains, it is also a good idea to have at least one pair of ruggedly constructed sunglasses made to one's prescription and in a protective case.

In high altitudes, sunglasses are so necessary that a spare pair in such areas is not a bad idea. This may be reasonably limited to one spare pair for the group. Incidentally, it is easier on the eyes to travel north on the long north-south trails when you have a choice.

A Magnifying Glass

A light little magnifying lens can be used during favorable weather to start a fire if you want, either when no quicker means is available or when it may be desirable to conserve matches.

One often comes in handy for odd functions, such as locating an imbedded thorn or splinter. There's also the fact that your trip is going to be for pleasure, and a magnifying glass works in well with many hobbies.

Some Kind of Mirror

It is not uncommon to get foreign matter in the eyes if the bush is at all thick or if one is traveling, for example, along an open ridge when there is a wind blowing up dust. Under such circumstances a hiker may have frequent use for a mirror.

There are also the numerous personal uses, and the fact that the mirror may also be useful in signaling. You may want to select a bright steel mirror weighing an ounce and a half and costing about a quarter postpaid.

Maps of the Territory

Maps come under the heading of necessity for intelligent and really enjoyable trail travel. They are inexpensive and easily obtainable. Sources are suggested in the first chapter of this book.

There are two basic ways to cut down weight and bulk with maps. The first is to trim off unnecessary portions. The second is to have maps waiting as you need them on an extended trip at post offices along the way. Get the largest scale you can reasonably come by, as this will make the task of planning and following your trip far easier.

Some Writing Materials

You will know best what you'll want. You might bring some good light paper, a few envelopes and stamps, and a ball-point pen with a fresh cartridge.

A lot of us like to make notes as we go along, perhaps in diary form. The handiest thing I have found for this is one of the little spiral-bound notebooks that fit into a shirt pocket. They are obtainable for about a dime.

The Books You Want

You may care to include a handbook on backpacking in your outfit. With such a compilation of fundamentals at hand for reference, it should be relatively easy to arrive at practical solutions for almost any number of hiking problems.

Then there are the one or more small hobby books you might like to bring along—something on astronomy, geology, botany, bird-watching, etc. Any hike will be more rewarding if you have some such side interest.

Then there are the books for just plain enjoyment, when you're relaxing at the day's end. One practical procedure is to take one book at a time, renewing this at supply points. It is often possible to swap books on the trail, and thus maintain a fresh supply.

Things in the Toilet Kit

This may include one small towel, or half a towel, that can be kept washed. Some hikers settle for just a face cloth. A hotel-sized cake of soap will generally do. It may be wrapped in the towel or in the face cloth, in a tiny oblong of plastic.

The kit may also include: toothbrush, dentifrice— unless you rely on something elsewhere in the outfit for this, perhaps using salt or baking soda—comb, nail file, sanitary supplies, and any small items you may want, such as a safety razor and blades.

Binoculars and Camera

Binoculars are not necessities by any means, but they can add so much to the scope and pleasure of a trip that, on some hikes at least, you may want to include them, possibly one small pair to a party.

A camera is not a necessity either, but it can make a lot of difference when you get back home and for years to come. There are numerous practical choices. My own is a 35mm. outfit with a lens brush, filters, a camera-holder that clamps into place on a rock or log and is far more compact than even a telescopic tripod, and an exposure meter. You'll want a tiny self-timer, so that when you're alone you can get into the picture.

A common problem is to have your camera loaded with black and white negative when you want to shoot color, or vice versa. Outside of a second camera in the party, if this is any problem with you, one answer is to carry your film in short loads. Then you're generally not committed too far in advance.

Some Lightweight Cord

A few yards of nylon cord, strong enough to support your weight in an emergency, will not take up much room. This always comes in handy in camp, especially if you carry a tarpaulin or plastic tube instead of a tent.

Most outfitters carry it at a few pennies a yard, weighing only a few ounces per length. It should preferably be kept in a cool, dry place, away from such organic compounds as gasoline and oil that attack synthetics.

A Good Insect Repellent

Having a supply of one of the more effective fly dopes in the kit can prevent a lot of annoyance in places and seasons where winged pests are prevalent.

The best commercial products available at this writing are those in which diethyl toluamide is an active ingredient. I had the opportunity of testing this raw product in the Far North, where the mosquitoes are thick enough to kill a man, mixing it with alcohol (which is its base in the finished products). I found that a solution stronger than the 50-50 blend formerly used by the army, and now by the commercial suppliers, was more effective. Army researchers have had similar experience, and the repellent now being used by the Department of the Army is made of 75 per cent diethyl toluamide and 25 per cent alcohol.

Your Snakebite Kit

In country where there are poisonous snakes, you should always have an adequate snakebite kit in your pocket. There is always the remote possibility that you may be bitten, and first aid would be highly essential.

There is a Cutter Hi-Lo Suction Snakebite Kit which takes up little more room than a 12-gauge shell and which answers excellently the demands of emergency treatment. Sporting goods dealers and drug stores handle these. Simply pocket the kit, which contains complete instructions, and don't worry. The mortaility from bites treated with such a kit is less than one per cent.

Flashlight, Bulb, and Batteries

A flashlight is always handy in and around camp. Although it is usually better to stop wherever you are long enough before dusk to set up a comfortable camp, this does not always work out; then the judicious, rather than the steady, use of a flashlight can help you get in safely. Although you can cut down weight considerably, if necessary, by picking a model with small batteries and a low-drain bulb, the familiar flashlight taking two size D batteries and a 50-ampere bulb is the most practical minimum.

These can be obtained in models as light as four ounces, with the batteries—which should be carried reversed in the cylinder to avoid accidental lighting in the pack—weighing about another five ounces apiece. The batteries to get are those made for heavy-duty, continuous-drain use for some five to ten times as long as the usual battery. You'll want an extra set, and all should be fresh at the start. You should also pack along a couple of spare bulbs, one of which it may be possible to pad with a dab of cotton and carry in the flashlight itself. I find a soft place for the other one is in my first aid kit.

The way to save flashlight power, of course, is by using it only in short spurts. If you have to travel by dark, on most trails you can get along better anyway with only brief flashes ahead to establish the pattern in your mind. Around a lot of camps, most of the time the campfire can be counted on to furnish all the necessary illumination, especially as one gets to live pretty much by the sun while in the wilderness.

Water Purifier Tablets

The easiest and most practical way to sterilize doubtful water, if you have a campfire, is to boil it. At or
near sea level, hard boiling for five minutes will do
the job. For every additional thousand feet of altitude, a safe all-around precaution is to increase the
boiling time one minute.

Or you can use halazone tablets, which may be
purchased at most sporting goods stores or at a drugstore. A small, two-ounce bottle containing a hundred
tablets costs about fifty cents and takes up less room
than a 12-gauge shell. Because this process depends
on the release of chlorine gas, the tablets should be
fresh and the container kept tightly closed.

Dissolve one table in a quart of water and let it
stand for half an hour. If the water is murky or particularly doubtful, both the time and the number of
tablets may well be doubled. Slosh a little of this
water over the lips of the container after the first few
minutes to sterilize these. Then cover the receptacle
as tightly as possible.

In Mexico and other semitropical and tropical regions, chlorine-releasing compounds cannot be de-
pended upon. Water there should either be boiled or,
when this is not convenient, treated with iodine water
purification tablets, available from drugstores.

Suntan Oils or Lotions

Heavy mineral oil, purchased under that name, is
about as good as any of the sunburn preventatives. It
is certainly the cheapest. The problem along the ma-

jor trails is one of altitude. The sun in tall country
burns right through ordinary tans built up at lower
levels. Furthermore, the type of lotions made most
for beach-goers is apt to have a rapidly evaporating
alcohol base.

The preventatives designed expressly for skiers are
a better bet. There are also special mountain-climbing
preparations, obtainable from the big catalog-issuing
dealers if not locally. Vulnerability differs widely,
and so do opinons. But the penalty is severe enough
that it's more prudent to overestimate the need for
protection. You may also want a chapstick.

Items in Repair Kits

The odds and ends of a painstakingly selected repair
kit will sometimes prove outrageously valuable in
proportion to their intrinsic worth in civilization. We
all have our own ideas about what a ditty bag of
such items should include. After years of adding and
discarding, here's what I now find in mine:

Large and small needles with matching nylon
thread. A hank of nylon fishline. A short length of
two-inch-wide nylon with adhesive on one side, that
can be used like adhesive tape on sleeping bags,
tents, and the like. A small tube of rubber cement
and a rectangle of rubber from which patches can be
cut for the air mattress. A one-ounce set of screw-
drivers, nesting within each other. Safety pins of various sizes, strung on the largest. An empty toothpaste
tube that, with the pitch from a conifer for flux, will
serve as emergency solder.

Pocket and Sheath Knives

A pocket knife with a single thin blade will admittedly serve many purposes. But most of us find that, particularly during ultralight travel, it is practical to add a sheath knife for the heavier tasks. A light blade five or six inches long works well for cutting boughs, getting some fuel, building shelters, and performing other tasks in the bush. A substantial sheath should be added for safety. If you don't want to carry it on your belt, it packs handily.

Although a good hand-crafted trail knife is quite expensive, you get what you pay for. Mine (a W. D. Randall knife) has stood by me in some rather strenuous pinches. It has a slim yet rugged six-inch blade and a light, unbreakable handle in which is set a small accurate compass—which is my emergency spare in case the regular compass ever becomes lost. In a snap pocket on the outside of the sheath is a little carborundum stone, with a medium grit on one side and a fine grit on the other, for keeping the blade sharp.

Your Stone Sharpener

A tiny light carborundum stone, preferably with a fine and a coarse side, is a necessity for keeping your cutting edges sharp. These little abrasive stones last so many years and are used so often that it's little wonder that some of them become more and more clogged with grime, progressively losing their effectiveness. To restore the cutting ability of your dirt-clogged carborundum, just put the stone in a good

bed of coals until it is red hot. Then it will be all
right again.

A Saw for Firewood

Indians used to make saws of bone and stone, and
with good reason. One can work up firewood much
more swiftly and easily, and with less risk, with a
saw designed for the purpose than with any ax or
hatchet. A number of portable saws are offered by
the sporting goods dealers. One particularly handy
and light variety consists of a blade that folds into a
steel handle. Other models are effectual too, and
weigh only a few ounces. You'll want a blade that's
toothed especially to cut firewood.

An Ax if You Need One

Although the ax is an almost indispensable tool for
the woodsman—many of whom rate it even above
matches as the most valuable item to have along in
the bush—one is very seldom necessary on a backpacking vacation. The one exception would be when
you are traveling in very cold weather and depending on night fires for warmth. If you do elect to take
an ax, perhaps for use in a base camp, the handiest
model for packing, although not for any great amount
of work, is the Hudson Bay model with a narrow butt
and a face of normal width.

This model, because of the narrow poll through
which the handle is attached, does not hold up too
well for heavy work. But for ordinary camping re-

quirements, where weight is a consideration and you still want an ax, a Hudson Bay with a one-and-a-half pound head and a twenty-four-inch handle will do a lot of jobs and will hold up for years. A metal-riveted leather sheath should ordinarily be added.

If you are going to be using a vacation ax very much, perhaps in a main camp from which you'll be hiking out most days, you will probably be more satisfied with an ordinary single-bit model with about a two-and-a-half-pound head. A handle about twenty-six to twenty-eight inches long is generally enough, though some find that they can swing the longer thirty-six-inch handle more naturally and therefore more safely. In any event, if you adopt one handle length and use it exclusively, you will come to do better and safer work.

Sometimes a Hatchet

The hatchet too is seldom necessary on a backpacking trip. Usually you can find and break up enough wood by hand for the limited cooking that's necessary. And generally, in the usual vacation weather, you should be able to depend on your sleeping bag to give you enough warmth at night without any fire.

There are exceptions, however, and some hikers like a light hand ax with about a twelve-inch handle. A number of these are available—one with a light hollow handle, to which water is added as needed to lend weight. Have a safe sheath for any hatchet, but don't ordinarily carry it on your belt. Most of the time this is both inconvenient and uncomfortable. Stow it instead in the packsack.

Nested Cooking Utensils

You'll need special cooking and eating paraphernalia. For the lone hiker, the practical minimum is two small kettles with covers—and with bails by which they can be hung over a fire—a frypan with a folding or detachable handle, a tablespoon, and a cup. The frying pan will serve as a plate, the cup as a bowl. One's pocket or sheath knife can be used whenever necessary.

Two nesting aluminum kettles, the larger holding about one-and-one-half quarts, together with an eight-inch frypan with conveniently folding handle, are available from dealers in camping goods. Weighing less than two pounds, they add no appreciable bulk to a pack inasmuch as food and other essentials can be stowed within them. Even when there are two or three people in the party, this same outfit can suffice; just add a plate, cup, and spoon for each individual.

Best of all for camping is a small nested cooking and eating outfit made of a light, tough aluminum compound. Anyone who has ever burned himself on aluminum will agree that the nested cups, and preferably the plates also, could just as well be of stainless steel. The frying pan should be stainless steel too.

I bought an outfit of this sort when I first started going into the real wilderness, and I've used it without replacements or changes ever since. As a matter of fact, many of the components are so handy that even in towns one or another of them is still used almost daily. There are several flimsy and highly impractical sets on the market. So buy your nested outfit, if you get one, from the best-established and most reliable sporting goods dealer with whom you can get in touch. Cost is surprisingly low.

Light fabric holders available for the pots and fry-pan permit their being cleanly packed without a lot of work scouring off the black every time. A few pieces of plastic sheeting will be even lighter. Actually, a certain amount of this exterior blackness makes for faster and more even cooking. When you get home, spots and discolorations on aluminumware can be removed with a solution made by dissolving a tablespoon of cream of tartar in a pint of water.

A durable set of nested aluminum measuring spoons takes up very little space and can be handy in both the kitchen and eating areas. There's not likely to be a regular measuring cup handy, so mark accurate proportions plainly on one of your drinking cups.

Plastic—in General

The simplest and handiest thing to take along for mixing and working purposes around food is a thin sheet of plastic. This can be easily washed, quickly refolded, and conveniently carried from one camping spot to another.

In fact, one of the most convenient things for each individual to carry when hiking is a thin sheet of lightweight plastic, perhaps five feet by seven feet. This will quickly fold into bandana handkerchief size, small enough for the pocket of a shirt. It can be drawn over one's head and shoulders as protection against wind and rain, laid atop the lower boughs of a tree as shelter from a storm, spread on the ground as an eating surface, and used as a clean waterproof wrapping for a string of sleek bright trout.

Foil Once in a While

Aluminum foil cookery is the modern version of enclosing food for cooking by bundling it in moist leaves, clay, or dripping green seaweed. The modern method encourages food to retain its juices and to warm evenly. Therein, as a matter of fact, lie the shortcomings. Meat wrapped in foil, for example, is steamed rather than roasted or broiled. The deliciously crisp brownness is missing. There are ways around it, of course. But these largely erase the virtues of simplicity.

A fish can be roasted directly on the coals if it is first wrapped in oiled foil; in the case of a small catch, you can impart a certain charred touch by toasting it unwrapped beforehand on a forked stick. With large fish, you can help along the taste by cooking bacon, dehydrated onion, and the like in the foil along with the fish.

Then there are the vegetables and such, when you are eating that first meal away from an outfitting post; their taste is not seriously impaired by this variety of cooking. The major drawback to any large amount of foil cookery, from the backpacker's viewpoint, is that its nature is more than of an occasional novelty. It does not really lend itself to serious cookery. Once in a while it's fun. But in the long run you save no time or energy. More importantly for go-light hikers on extended trips, you also save no weight.

You May Need a Stove

The one-burner primus stove is often the answer for campers who hike beyond the tree line, although if you're in and out without doing any serious climbing, it's often possible to pack wood instead. In any event, these light, efficient little stoves may be obtained in functional units burning kerosene, gasoline, or canned gas. Alcohol is not generally adequate, burning with too cool a flame.

For example, there is a two-and-a-half pound combination selling for about fifteen dollars which includes: a three-and-a-half-pint casserole; a two-and-a-half-pint casserole; one lid pan; one upper and lower wind-guard; a potholder; a strap; and a gasoline stove—all nesting in a space eight-and-a-quarter inches in diameter and four-and-three-quarter inches high. Lightweight, leakproof aluminum fuel bottles are also inexpensively available. The big catalog-issuing camp equipment dealers stock a functional variety of these units and combinations.

Things for Dishwashing

A little scouring pad and a supply of detergent, carried perhaps in a plastic container and renewed at each supply point, will make a lot of difference in dishwashing. A small, tough cellulose sponge can take the place of a dishcloth.

Include Your Canteen

This is necessary on most trails not only for carrying water, which may be fairly plentiful, but for use as a container in which a doubtful drinking supply can be kept purified by the use of halazone or some other such preparation.

Both plastic and aluminum have proved themselves in this department. I like one where the cap is safely on a chain.

Salt and Pepper

A number of different containers are readily available for carrying salt and pepper on the trail. If you select aluminum, make sure it is treated to prevent corrosion. When you don't use pepper, there isn't much use in filling that compartment. I use mine instead for water purification tablets or sometimes, in hot country, for salt tablets.

Vitamins for Long Hikes

The usually balanced diet supplies all the vitamins necessary. However, it is true that in many cases the capacity of the body to store these is meager. Although actual deficiency diseases are very unlikely to overtake hikers, the earlier symptoms of deficiency —such as undue irritability—can foreseeably appear. Therefore, on any extended hike with dehydrated rations, carrying vitamin pills can be a reasonable precaution. For the same reason, in such circumstances a mineral supplement may as well be included.

Whistles for Signaling

Whistles can be useful for keeping a group together, attracting help, sending messages, and for other purposes when they will serve better than shouts.

A Small Can Opener

You are perhaps unlikely to carry any canned goods requiring openers except for certain brands of dehydrated products. But various such foods obtainable at stores along the routes provide welcome treats and vacations from cooking before you go on again. This means you may want a can opener. A handy one is the little folding variety, weighing about one-eighth of an ounce and costing about fifteen cents, which can be tucked into a watch pocket or somewhere equally handy for when you want to dip into that cool can of peaches.

Certainly Your Fishing Gear

If you hike very far, you're apt to be passing through some wonderful fishing country, well back from the roads, where there will be not only great sport but also gourmet food. Fine rods and reels, made expressly for go-light trips, are so compact and comparatively weightless than if your current budget has room for it, you should certainly get a set.

At the very least get a small container, perhaps an aluminum 35mm. color film case, and fit in a few hooks, flies, and perhaps either some split shot or some tiny strips of lead that can later be twisted into place as sinkers. You may want to include some salmon eggs for bait. You won't forget, either, to wind a small quantity of light, durable fishline such as nylon on a piece of cardboard, figuring to cut a pole on the spot.

Don't Forget Anything

What you take on your hike is pretty much a personal matter. The main thing is not to drive off and leave some wanted item behind. There are at least a couple of ways to avoid that disaster.

One way is to make a check list with a separate column for each group of essentials. One column will be for clothing, a second for food, another for sleeping gear, and so on.

Tape or clip this list to a piece of cardboard. Use it during preparations of course, but also have it on hand when you pack for the start. At that decisive moment, recheck items one by one as a preventative measure against going off and forgetting some indispensable item.

A second method, for those who have ample space, is to use the visual technique of building little piles. Place tentage in one group, dining and cooking utensils in another, and so on. When a certain article is in use at the moment, or needs to be picked up at the store or removed from the refrigerator, a note to that effect weighed down in the proper pile will serve as a handy reminder.

Keep a record for future reference—note what is left *unused* at the end of your journey. This information will be very helpful when you outfit for your next sojourn into the wilderness.

7/Modern Hiker's First Aid Kit

E. Russel Kodet, M.D.

Reprinted from *Outdoor Life*. Copyright © 1962, Popular Science Publishing Co., Inc.

Special Kits for Backpackers

Treatment for Lacerations and Scratches

Equipment for Taking Stitches

A Supply of Tape and Gauze

Medicines for Eye Injuries

A Supply of Empirin

Drugs for Major Infections

Lomotil and Sulfasuxidine

A Packet of Pyridium

How to Get Your Supply of Drugs

The Approximate Cost of Supplies

The Over-All Kit Expense

7

Special Kits for Backpackers

Because I am a doctor, I am interested in having a personal first aid kit that I know to be adequate for any problem I am likely to encounter in my outings. Because I also like to backpack, I am interested in reducing weight to an absolute minimum. With these two interests in mind, I have assembled a first aid kit that can be used to treat everything from a case of dysentery to a laceration, and it weighs less than four ounces.

With people having more and more leisure time, and growing numbers of us seeking remote areas on our hunting, fishing, and camping trips, the need for a good first aid kit—such as I have and am about to describe—is becoming increasingly important. A lot of time, money, and effort can go into planning and making a trip, and all too often a mishap or illness can ruin the whole thing.

I realize I may be criticized by some of my medical colleagues for suggesting a do-it-yourself kit for serious injuries. I want to make it clear that medical attention should be sought for injuries other than minor ones, but if such attention cannot be obtained, preparations must be made to provide for emergency treatment and to prevent needless discomfort. This first aid kit is not intended for the Sunday picnicker.

The items in my kit are not what the average fellow would carry. This is an important point. The average person carries a lot of worthless bulk, and nine times out of ten does the wrong thing with what he does have. I see daily evidences of this in my practice. If a fellow is going to the trouble of carrying a kit, then he should have an effective one. While the contents of the one I suggest are not so readily procurable as those of the conventional type, they are well worth the effort of getting them. You'll need some prescriptions from your doctor, and you can get the supplies from your druggist or a surgical supply house. None of them is hard to obtain.

You will note that, with the exception of eyedrops, the kit contains no liquids because of their tendency to be heavy and to spill.

Treatment for Lacerations and Scratches

Lacerations and scratches are probably the most common results of outdoor accidents. There is no place for the use of alcohol, Merthiolate, or similar antiseptics in these injuries, though year after year first aid books tell you to douse wounds liberally with them. It is true that these substances kill germs, but they also kill tissue, and using them in open wounds will devitalize (kill) tissue. Because germs grow best in devitalized tissue, and some germs are always present, you can see that these preparations set the stage for a future wound infection. At the very least, they delay rather than hasten healing.

The best way to handle a cut or scrape is to wash it well with plenty of soap and water, dry it well, and apply a dressing. Since I have soap elsewhere, I do not carry it in the kit. If the wound is oozy and you feel the dressing might stick to it, a plastic-like absorbent tissue called Telfa should be put over the wound first and then covered with a gauze flat. Telfa can be bought in different sizes in sterile packages in any drugstore. No dressing will ever stick when it is used. *Never use an ointment on a wound unless it is already infected.*

If the wound is gaping, it will have to be brought together. This is done most easily with a butterfly. A butterfly is a plastic tape which is applied across the laceration to pull and hold the edges together. This will suffice in most cases. For deep cuts in fingers and other places subject to much movement, a stitch may be better. Everyone should be immunized against tetanus (lockjaw) *before* suffering an injury. Tetanus is a dreadful disease and, although it is not common, can occur from even a trivial injury.

Equipment for Taking Stitches

If a person is far from a doctor, it behooves him to know the rudiments of taking a stitch, or suture. This is done without Novocain. Nerves are often cut along with the skin, and the pain of the sewing needle is not so bad as one would think. I have sewed lacerations on myself and my children in this manner. The fuss and special techniques required to handle syringes, needles, and Novocain do not justify their use in a first aid kit of this type. Sure, it hurts for just a second when a stitch is taken, but it is easier to bear this than to seek out a doctor's office when you are in a remote place, to say nothing of ruining a trip looking for one.

A sterile suture package can be bought with the nylon thread joined to the end of a cutting needle. I use size 3-0 for everything except the face. Though 5-0 is finer and has less tendency to leave a scar, either size is O.K. The cut is first washed with soap and water, dried, and then sutured. The needle is held with a small mosquito clamp (also called a hemostat). This clamp is a miniature, self-locking, needle-nosed plier. It is also useful in extracting slivers (especially from under a fingernail), fishhooks, thorns, and so on. And it can be used for repair jobs. I remember when the spring of my spinning-reel bail came out of its socket once on a fishing trip. The small mosquito clamp was the only way to hold it and slip it back into its recess.

Once the stitch is taken, the suture is tied and cut with the scalpel blade. The ends are left a quarter of an inch long to facilitate removal in seven days. The clamp can substitute as a pair of tweezers to pull the severed stitch out. Any bleeding that occurs from the wound usually stops when the stitch is taken, or with direct, steady pressure over the wound for five to ten minutes.

The suture is taken through the skin. The stitch is taken only through the skin, never deeper into the underlying fat or muscle. Anyone who has ever skinned an animal will readily visualize the thickness of skin, which is never more than a quarter of an inch. When one does not go any deeper, no vital structure will ever be encountered. The only possible source of difficulty might be in hitting a blood vessel.

If this happens, simply pull the suture through and out of the skin and take it in another spot a little above or below the one that caused the trouble. The bleeding will always stop with pressure for a minute or so. One word of caution: *never suture close to an eyelid*. The healing may pull the skin into a distorted position and cause later difficulties. I can appreciate that the taking of a stitch sounds formidable, but it is really quite simple.

In snake country I carry a set of suction cups. The scalpel blades serve as the lancets.

A Supply of Tape and Gauze

I find that instead of buying half-inch tape in one strip, it is better to buy half-inch tape split in half so it comes off the spool as two quarter-inch strips. The latter makes a neater dressing, saves tape, and can be used double if needed to supply half-inch widths.

Kling roller gauze is better than regular gauze because it sticks to itself by its fibers, which interlock. No adhesive is necessary, and it is a pleasure to use. Band-Aids are best with the new Super-Stick adhesive.

Medicines for Eye Injuries

The other items in my recommended kit are included because of past experiences or possible future emergencies. Don't let their jaw-breaking names discourage you. Copy them down, or perhaps take this book with you when you ask your doctor for the needed prescriptions or drugs.

One evening several years ago, when I was on a

fishing trip in a remote area, I was tying a lure onto
my line. The rod was bent under the pressure of my
pulling the line taut. Suddenly the line slipped, and
the pole snapped into my glasses. The glasses shat-
tered, and I got an eyeful of glass. I spent a very
miserable night waiting for daylight to seek help. I
now carry a mixture of Pontocaine and Neohydeltrasol
mixed in equal parts. This is a local anesthetic for the
eye, plus a neomycincortisone mixture for the treatment of infection or inflammation of the eyes. This is
the thing to use if the eye is hit by a flying wood chip
or anything similar. One drop each three hours suf-
fices. It will also give immediate relief in snow blind-
ness, often got at high atltitudes. Because the
Pontocaine anesthetizes it, the eye has lost its protective sensitivity and wink reflexes. So stay out of windy
places after using it, and do not touch the eye. Better
yet, wear a patch over the eye for two hours after
putting in the drops; their effect is about gone by
then.

A Supply of Empirin

Empirin Compound is a must; it is more effective
than aspirin. Many people get high-altitude head-
aches at elevations over six to seven thousand feet,
and the caffein in Empirin helps overcome the
drowsiness that often occurs at these heights. No caffein is present in aspirin. Empirin is also useful in any
condition involving the skin, muscles, bones, and
joints. It also relieves the discomfort of sunburn, skin
itching, sprains, and so on. It has no effect on pain
arising from the inner organs of the abdomen or chest.

Drugs for Major Infections . . .

Nausea, vomiting, or intestinal cramps respond nicely to either one 5mg. Compazine tablet every three to four hours, or one Tridol each four hours. If vomiting continues, however, seek help.

Generally sickness is a rarity on wilderness trips. But the kit contains a three-day supply of both penicillin and Achromycin for use in major infections. Because these drugs are expensive, one is usually enough. This is sufficient to handle a case of blood poisoning, pneumonia, or any other severe infection. Have your doctor prescribe them for you and tell you how to use them.

Lomotil and Sulfasuxidine

There is always the possibility of consuming tainted food or water, either in a restaurant when traveling or in the wilderness. I used to carry paregoric. It worked well, but it is a liquid and subject to spillage. A new drug called Lomotil avoids this problem. It is supplied in 2.5mg. tablets, and the dose is one every two to four hours for diarrhea. A dozen tablets should be enough to take along. I also carry Sulfasuxidine in the same bottle. These sterilize the intestine of bacteria and are used in doses of two or three every four to six hours. It takes several days for them to do their job.

A Packet of Pyridium

My kit also contains a small packet of Pyridium. Some people, women especially, are subject to bladder infections and can be miserable with them. In our family it is the basset hound that always seems to get one of these attacks far from anywhere. When he is miserable, he sees to it that we are kept miserable too. The Pyridium tablets provide complete urinary anesthesia if one is taken every four to six hours.

How to Get Your Supply of Drugs

All the drugs except the Empirin require a doctor's prescription. There are very few effective drugs available without a prescription any more because of the federal laws governing the sale of drugs over the counter.

Getting a prescription or having one called into the drugstore should present no problems if you call your doctor and explain what you want and how you want to use it. Most doctors would be happy to oblige if they knew the drugs would not be used indiscriminately. Your doctor may even give you many of them at no cost from samples which he constantly receives.

The Approximate Cost of Supplies

The nylon suture material packaged with the attached needle can be bought in any surgical supply house for $.60, scalpel blades for .10 each, and the special clamp I described for about $3.00. A pair of small needle-nosed pliers could substitute for the clamp. All gauze, Telfa, and the dressings can be bought in any drugstore at nominal cost.

Twelve penicillin or Achromycin capsules should be adequate for any severe infection. Their cost is $.50 each, making them the most expensive item in the kit. The Sulfasuxidine tablets are .05 each, Compazine .08, Tridol, .06, and Lomotil .15. If weight is no problem, paregoric is cheaper. Local cost may vary somewhat. The Pontocaine-Neohydeltrasol prescriptions will run about $4.00. If the Pontocaine alone is used with the Neohydeltrasol, relief of pain and discomfort will be achieved for .50 (quarter-ounce bottle). No antibiotic will then be in the mixture however.

The Over-All Kit Expense

The total cost of the kit would then vary between $10.00 and $20.00, depending on whether one uses the special clamp, the Neohydeltrasol, and the Lomotil. It would go something like this: clamp, $3.00; the bandages, etc., $1.00; penicillin or Achromycin, $6.00; Sulfasuxidine, $2.00; Neohydeltrasol-Pontocaine, $4.00; Lomotil, $2.00; Compazine .40; Tridol .30; and suture .60.

This may seem expensive, but when you consider that a simple hunt or trip costs over several hundred dollars for travel and much more for equipment, then in its true perspective this kit is not out of line. Nothing comes cheap, least of all good equipment. Injuries and sickness are never bargained for, and one can always find better things to do with the money for drugs until they are really needed. Then they are worth much more.

All the drugs are stable and will last indefinitely, except the antibiotics. These should be replaced every two or three years. Ask your druggist when the penicillin or Achromycin should be renewed.

There you have it. Like any fisherman's tackle box,

it will gradually be changed over the years or to suit certain circumstances. I have been using this kit for several years now and am well satisfied with it. When I am not traveling in remote areas from my home in Shafter, California, I keep it in my car so it is always handy.

8/ Enjoy the Trail You Take

Get Yourself in Condition
Maintain a Comfortable Pace
Rest at the Right Times
Walk in the Easiest Way
Know Where You Are . . .
Finding Direction by the Sun
Finding Direction with a Compass
Always Stay Found

8

Get Yourself in Condition

You needn't make any conditioning preparations at all if you don't want to, getting gradually into shape on the trail itself instead. After all, this is going to be a pleasure stroll. Even the fixed camps on the big routes are reasonably close together, and you can always set your own pace, camping in between if some spot beckons.

Age and basic physical condition need to be considered. With exercise it is possible to get in good hiking condition well within a week if there is a hale basis on which to build. Even older and softer individuals find that the longer they hike without undue pressing today, the farther they will be able to hike tomorrow.

If one is able to walk, he will be able to hike. The trails these days attract both youngsters and oldsters. After all, no one is obliged to make an endurance test out of what can be just a pleasant stroll. The aim is to enjoy getting from one camp to the other. There is no record sheet of elapsed times.

Conditioning was in many ways less of a problem, of course, before the days of instant transportation.

The best conditioning today for a backpacking journey is still walking—preferably on hard, strenuous,
regular jaunts. Especially if you're going to be taking
one of the mountain trails, hit as many hills beforehand as possible, even to the point of monotony. A
good stunt if you happen to live near a stadium is to
climb up and down the stairs for increasing periods
each day. In fact, any stairs will do.

Weeks of calisthenics are especially good for those
forced into largely sedentary living. It helps some individuals to keep a chart; so many knee-bends, leg-
lifts, pushups, etc. Then the competitive spirit urges
one both to continue the daily sessions and to improve
past performances. Not enough spare time? Try filling
in a favorite news program this way. Keep it up.

The better condition you're in when you start, the
better time you'll have on your backpacking vacation.

Maintain a Comfortable Pace

This is a highly individual matter, although it is generally flexible enough to be moderated to fit a party's
average rate of travel. The main thing is not to press.
The best test of an ideal pace is that you can hold it
all day.

This does not mean that you'll necessarily walk at
the same speed for the entire day. In the chill of the
morning, I personally like to go out fast to keep warm
rather than to burden myself with extra clothing that
will become too hot later on. After lunch, I usually
have another spurt of energy, slackening off in the
afternoon until the thoughts of that next camp
quicken my steps again along toward the end of that
particular hiking day. The main thing is not to make

a chore out of any of it, but rather to see what's happening about you and to enjoy yourself to the fullest along the way.

Rest at the Right Times

How about rests? Often it will be enough just to lean against a tree or rock for a few minutes in such a way that the weight of the pack is taken off your shoulders. Perhaps half an hour after you start you may want a complete halt to adjust that belt and those shoelaces, to get a drink, and to refresh yourself generally. Another full stop in midmorning may be what you need to take you over the miles between that point and lunch. Some hikers prefer not to stop even at noon. Again it's a matter of choice; I've nearly always found that a full stop at midday with a hot lunch, usually toasted sandwiches, and a pail of hot tea makes the afternoon far shorter and more pleasant. In most instances you should make camp when there's still plenty of daylight.

The one thing to avoid is the sort of prolonged rest that lets you get cold and stiff and consequently makes the remaining miles really tough. These are a real danger when you're pressing hard and fast. In ordinary going where you keep well within your capacities, there is ordinarily little danger if you always start traveling again while you're still warm.

This doesn't mean that an occasional taste of the really rough sort of traveling isn't refreshing too—because aching legs and laboring lungs usually have a few more miles left in them, and also the human frame increases its efficiency most quickly when it is driven closest to its limits.

Sure, rough it if you want to prove to yourself th
(actually very important) fact that you can rough i
One day, it's true, anyone at all may be thrown er
tirely upon his own resources and forced to get alon
the best he can with a minimum of bodily comfor
But as far as the preference goes, roughing it is
development stage. Once we've successfully teste
our ability to take it, a whole lot of doubts and inhib
tions disappear. We find ourselves realizing that th
real challenge lies in smoothing it. We come to appre
ciate that making it easy on ourselves takes a lot mor
experience and ingenuity than bulling it through th
tough way.

Walk in the Easiest Way

These mechanized years more and more of us ar
forgetting how to walk. This is so generally true tha
perhaps a few refresher hints may not be out of orde
for those weeks when your daily stroll will be farthe
than from car to door.

Most of us find that we can maintain better, an
therefore safer, balance by keeping the feet pointe
as nearly straight ahead as is comfortable. A lot c
hikers also find it is not too tiring to come up on th
toes, thus gaining both impetus and distance.

On one of the designated trails it is better to follov
the trail, if only to avoid the resulting erosion that i
apt to result from the practice of detouring betwee
switchbacks. But on side trips it may be well to re
member that it usually requires a disproportionat
amount of energy to travel straight up and dow
hills, as the trails of animals show they well know. W

will generally do better in the long run either to zig-zag or to slant off at a gradual pitch.

A sensible formula to repeat and to heed whenever walking in the wilderness is: Never step on anything you can step over, and never step over anything you can step around.

Know Where You Are . . .

No one is going to feel confident, relaxed, and utterly at home in the wilderness unless he understands the few very simple principles of finding his way anywhere and, whether on a main route's well-blazed trail or not, of always knowing where he is.

There is nothing at all difficult about finding your way through strange wilderness, always knowing the direction back to the main trail, and never getting lost. It is downright easy, in fact, for staying found is just a matter of common sense and of keeping your wits about you.

But, first, let's disabuse ourselves of the commonest of the utterly false notions that have been formed about this all-important part of woodcraft. No man is born with the ability to find his way out and back through country entirely strange to him. The prowess is acquirable; it is not instinctive.

Neither does any human being carry a compass in his head. Even the most intuitive native, who has spent all his years in wild places, can find his way without outside help only through regions with which he is already familiar.

The educated individual, although he may have been born in the city and lived there most of his life, often makes a far better explorer than a native, as has been proved innumerable times. One reason for this is the fact that knowing where you're going, being sure of where you are, and always having the certain knowledge of how to get back is no mysterious matter of instinct and mumbo jumbo. It is, on the contrary, a positive and ever intriguing problem of distances and angles.

Finding Direction by the Sun

The sun and moon have always risen in the east and set in the west. Everyone knows that at midday (sun time) in the United States and Canada the sun is to the south, and that at midnight so is the full moon. Any time either the sun or the moon is bright enough to cast a shadow, there is a rough way to determine direction. Mark the tip of a pole's shadow. Wait five minutes or so. Then a straight line drawn from the shadow's new tip through the first mark will run roughly west.

The new moon, with its concavity to the left, is in the west in early morning. The old moon is in the east. The moon, like the stars and the sun, rises in the east and sets in the west.

The two outer stars that form the bowl of the Big Dipper point to the North Star, which has the appearance of being about seven times as far from them as they are from each other.

Finding Direction with a Compass

The only difficulty with these ways of reckoning comes in cloudy, stormy, foggy, and otherwise obscure weather. Then everyone in strange and unmarked country, unless he is going to camp until the weather clears, is going to need a magnetic compass.

As you no doubt already know, using a compass is a very simple matter. In the United States and Canada, if you place a magnetic compass away from metal on a flat surface and let the needle settle down, it will point north. That is, it will point toward the magnetic north. This is a shifting point above Hudson Bay in extreme northeastern Canada, almost due north of Ohio. In the State of Washington the needle points east of true north about twenty degrees. In Maine the declination runs about twenty degrees west.

Although this is not technically exact, it is in general enough for everyday travel. Actually, the entire earth is a magnet, causing the declination to vary at different spots. In some localities this may be as much as fifteen degrees away from the magnetic shift indicated on ordinary maps.

To determine the local declination from true north, find the North Star. This lies almost exactly over the North Pole, varying only slightly more than one degree from precise north. You can then note immediately the variation between almost exact north and where your compass needle is pointing. Or you can scratch a line pointing to this Pole Star, or indicate it with two stakes, and in daylight compare your compass to this north-south mark.

The declination must be taken into consideration when you're reading a map. As a matter of fact, it is marked on many maps. If no compass directions are shown on the particular map you are using, true north may be assumed to be at the top, this being the way most maps are laid out.

Always Stay Found

There are two kinds of maps. One is the "mind" map which you keep in your head as you go along. The other is the more or less accurate published map.

Your mind map, plus plain ordinary common sense, will keep you from getting turned around or lost. If for any reason whatsoever you have the slightest doubt of being able to retain this map accurately in your head (and ordinarily this does take practice), then just sketch it on a piece of paper as you go along.

This is the entire secret of finding your way and not getting lost. You must always know where you have gone and, by this knowledge, always know approximately where you are. This is not nearly so complex as it may sound. In fact, it is not complicated at all. You merely keep oriented and, using a watch, keep count of how far in point of time you go in each direction. Every ten minutes or every time you change direction will not, at first, be too often to bring that map up to date.

Whenever you know where you have been and where you are, you will always know the way back. That's all there is to it.

A final tip. If you camp by a river, for example, don't try to return to camp in a direct line after a day of exploring. Instead, bear definitely to one side or the other. Then upon reaching the river you'll know for sure which way to turn.

9/Enjoy the Fires You Build

9

The Fondest Memories

What remain most fondly in our mind after a wilderness hike are the campfires. The handful of twigs that boil the kettle at noon. The cooking coals at the end of the day, when you can hardly wait for that dehydrated steak or flaky trout. The flames behind whose sanctuary you sit while the darkening forest comes to life.

Then there is that first fire at dawn. Because of air currents set into motion by the blending of day and night, it's colder now than it was during total darkness. The cook of the morning maybe deposits an old pine stump, saved for the purpose, in the center of the fading overnight embers. This gives him a blaze like the light of a pressure lantern—and it also helps him to get some warmth into his extended fingers. Pretty soon he's thawed out enough to shove the coffee pot grumpily into the heat. He then begins banging pans around a little more expressively than necessary. Further sleep soon becomes impossible. The coffee smells too good anyway, particularly when joined by the aromas of flapjacks and bacon.

Much of the success of a hiking trip, as well as a

considerable deal of the pleasure, is going to depend
on your having the right kinds of cooking fires. This
does not mean that campfires, if those are what you
use, should be built in just one way. It all depends
upon where you are, what you have, and whether
your most pressing needs at the moment are for tea,
chops, or mouth-tingling stew.

Regulating the Open Fire

When conditions are favorable, trail meals never taste
better than when they are prepared over the red
gleaming warmth of wild wood. It's so easy to regulate
the open cooking fire so as to take advantage of
quickly roaring heat, or to provide a bed of coals that
will break apart for broiling, or to conjure up such
fringe benefits that a dumpling-festooned mulligan
will either simmer or just keep temptingly warm.

When you want to start those food smells tantaliz-
ing your sensibilities in a hurry, the various dry soft
woods, especially when split, will quickly flare into a
blaze. For steadier and more conservative heat, the
hard woods are more satisfactory. For an enduring
expanse of glowing coals, you will probably choose,
when possible, such fuels as oak, hickory, and ash.
Or perhaps, if you're back in sheer wilderness, you'll
split up one of the sweet black-smoking birches with
its tendency to get extremely hot even when green.

Although campfires can be made in numerous ways,
the principles remain the same. An understanding of
these renders fire-making under every practical cir-
cumstance a lot more easy. Firewood, for one thing,
does not itself actually burn. A gas driven from the
wood by heat is what flames. To be capable of this,

the gas must first combine with the oxygen in the air.

What we need for a campfire, therefore, is fuel that is sufficiently flammable to give off combustible gas in sufficient quantity to be lit by the heat we are able to concentrate on it. This initial fire, in turn, must be hot and lasting enough to release and ignite more and more gas from progressively larger fuel.

Starting Your Fire

If birch is growing around your camp, the very best kindling will be birch bark. Unless you're in a heavily frequented area, enough small shreds of this can be pulled off by hand so there will be no need, even deep in the woods, to disfigure the tree.

In evergreen country you needn't ever have difficulty in starting a blaze in any kind of weather. A fairly tight handful of the dead resinous twigs that abound in the lower parts of conifers will readily burst into flame at the touch of a match. The only exception occurs in damp cold weather. Then freezing moisture sometimes sheaths the forest with ice. When this happens, the solution still remains simple. You only have to expose the dry oily interiors of the dead branches.

Shavings from pitch pine light very easily. So do shavings from any dry wood you find adhering to standing evergreens. If no soft wood is about, look for dead wood on other trees. If you do have to use fallen litter for kindling, be sure that what you choose is firm and dry.

Fuzzsticks, when you need to bother with them, start a fire quickly. They are made by shaving a piece of wood again and again, not detaching the accumulating curls. These fuzzsticks are commonly employed instead of paper, by the way, to start stove fires in the backwoods. Light fuzzsticks and all other kindling so that the flames will be able to eat upward into the fresh fuel.

One way to start a campfire, then, is to bunch a few wisps of birch bark on the bare ground. Pile a handful of small, dry evergreen twigs above this. Over this lean a few larger, seasoned conifer twigs. Also, in wigwam fashion so that ample oxygen will reach all parts of the fuel, lay up some dead hard wood. Then ignite the birch bark so the flames will eat into the heart of the pile. Once the fire gets going well, you can shape it any way you want.

The lighting should almost always be accomplished with a single match, even on those occasions when plenty of matches are at hand. This slowly acquired skill may on some later day mark the difference between a warmly comfortable camp and a chilly and miserably damp one.

The ordinary wooden matches are best. These should be held so that any draft reaching them will feed the fire down the stem, where it will be able to keep burning. This you will accomplish in whatever way seems best at the moment. You may face the wind with both hands cupped in front of the flaming match. You may stretch out between the breeze and the carefully heaped flammables so that your body will act as a shield. You may use your jacket or any other handy article, such as a large sheet of bark, to protect the first feeble flames.

There is no time in any wooded area when a campfire cannot thus be built from materials at hand. You can always either find or make a sheltered nook. Even when a cold rain is freezing as it falls, shavings and kindling can be provided with a knife. If you do not have a suitable knife, you can still shatter and splinter enough dead wood with which to kindle a blaze. If (preferably) birch bark is available from a dead tree, one sheet will form a dry base on which to arrange campfire makings, while other sheets angled about and above will keep off moisture until the fire is crackling.

Equipping Your Cooking Fire

When an experienced hiker merely wants to get water boiling in his tea pail and toast a sandwich or two, he builds a small fire in the easiest way he can, depending on what fuel is nearby. Then he cuts a green stick several feet long. This tea stick he shoves into the ground so that one end extends over the heat. He may adjust its height by propping it up with a rock, chunk of wood, or forked stick. If the ground is hard, he may weigh down the lower end with a billet or stone.

The pail he hangs by its bail at the end of the tea stick. The surface of this stick is generally rough enough so that the handle won't slide. Also, branches are so trimmed that a few projections remain. If necessary, a notch can very easily be cut. Incidentally, a practical tea pail is often only a large can with two opposite holes punched near its rim to accommodate a makeshift wire handle.

A larger meal is often prepared with the help of additional angled green poles. However, the round fire is generally not too convenient for cooking purposes. One answer is to arrange a number of such

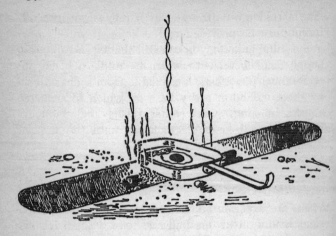

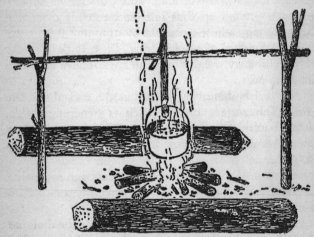

TYPICAL CAMPFIRES FOR COOKING.

Above—Trench fire arrangement. Below—Cooking fire between two logs.

small fires of varying intensities, just as you use different burners on a city range.

But the problem becames one of most easily supporting the various cooking utensils. As usual, solutions are numerous. One handy method that will do away with a lot of teetering and tipping is to scoop, scrape, or stamp a trench. This may be about six inches wide and deep and perhaps two feet long. Running this trench in the same direction as the wind will assure a better draft. Get a good fire going in this trench, perhaps by raking it there after it gets blazing well. Then kettle, frypan, and pots can be steadied across it. Such a fire, however, probably won't be too successful if either the day is quiet or the fuel is none too ardent.

The answer may then be the more usual aboveground fire, but one that's some eight inches wide and four or five feet long. This fire may be contained by two fairly dry logs some four to six inches in diameter, laid either parallel or at a slight angle with the open end toward the wind. If these logs are raised an inch or two by stones or billets, air will be able to circulate advantageously beneath them. Fuel this fire with preferably long split hardwood, and, if possible, let it burn down either to a hot bed of coals or to a steady blaze which does not flame up more than a foot.

Meanwhile, cut two substantial forked green sticks. Drive these upright into the ground at each end of the fire so that a green crosspiece laid between the crotches will extend the length of the center of the fire. Make pothooks for each kettle by cutting handle-holding notches in forked sticks that can be inverted over this crosspiece.

A convenient variation of this technique is to use two green poles on either side of the fire, instead of the somewhat seasoned logs. Take pains to raise these evenly above the ground, perhaps notching the supporting billets if that's what you're using. Such green poles will take a long time to burn through. Just set your cooking utensils across them.

Distracting the Smoke

Ever notice how smoke seems to follow you around a campfire? Matter of fact, it actually does follow you. The reason for this is that smoke is pulled into the partial vacuum made by any nearby object. The way out is to create a larger attraction than that of your person. One method of doing this is by building the fire against a boulder or sandy bank. Or locate some other bulk or surface nearby but at a safe distance.

Observing Safety Rules

Find out about fire regulations in advance and get any necessary fire permits. Some regions allow campfires only in prescribed locations. In any event, it does not pay to take chances with a fire. Never kindle one on surfaces made up largely of decomposed and living vegetation. Fire will sometimes eat deeply into such footing. An individual may think he has put it out; but unseen and unsuspected, it may smolder for days and weeks. It may lie nearly dormant during an entire winter. With the warmth and increasing dryness of spring, it may regain new vigor, until one hot day a strong wind can cause it to erupt into a devastating forest fire.

When you leave a camp or bivouac in a potentially dangerous area for more than a few minutes, put out that fire. *Saturate it with water.* Stir the ground beneath and around it, working and soaking ashes and dust into mud. Dig around it until you are certain no root or humus will lead the blaze away like a fuse. Feel with your hands to make sure that all heat has been safely diminished. Examine the vicinity for any activity resulting from sparks and flying embers.

10/Food for the Farthest Places

10

Food That Tastes Good

When your appetite is sharpened by the sort of out-door living for which human beings were made, the mealtimes can include some of the best moments of any vacation—if you outfit yourself with foods that keep well, cook readily, and are easy to handle.

Now is not too soon to get started on your provisioning for that hike back of beyond; because, done right, it's going to take some time. You'll do best to take foods you personally like and know how to prepare. Experimenting at home and on weekend journeys is the soundest way to find out how much of each item you'll need to round out the sort of satisfying meals that will keep you going under full power.

Nothing is more important on a hike than the grub. Most of us go into the farther places to have a good time. If the victuals are poor, unwholesome, not what we crave, we have a continuous grouch. If they are appetizing and there's plenty of everything, all is rosy. Satisfying food even makes up for rain and hard beds. Good fellowship is at its best around good meals.

Far from the humdrum concerns of man-made civilization, it is possible as nowhere else to appreciate the simple pleasures of life—the browning frypan bread, steaming coffee, and bacon sputtering over the coals. The crackle of your campfire takes on an unexpected coziness, and even the smallest tent all at once seems as snug and satisfying as a mansion.

The Basic Grubstakes

The standard foods taken by experienced outdoorsmen on hikes into the farther places of this continent, and which in general form the basis of many grubstakes, include: flour, baking powder, sugar, compact cereals such as quickly cooking rice and oatmeal, corn meal, side bacon which has nearly triple the calories of back bacon, oleomargarine, salt, spaghetti and such, powdered milk and eggs, dried fruits and vegetables, and other dehydrated foods. All these are practically free of water.

Some of the more nutritious spreads such as honey, jam, and peanut butter work in well. So does cheese.

Practical beverages are concentrated tea powder or tea itself, one of the instant coffees, malted milk, and chocolate. Bouillon solids and dry soup mixes, although short on nourishment, are often welcome because of the easy variety they afford. Seasonings such as powdered onion, pepper, a favorite spice or two, as well as a few extracts, may be desirable.

Well-Proportioned Quantities

No one can give you more than an idea of the quantities to take of various items. Detailed grub lists as such are ordinarily of little value, for they seldom suit anyone but the compiler. It all depends on the number of meals you expect to make of each food, how many are to be in the party, and how much of that particular nutriment it will take to make a satisfying portion for each individual concerned.

To determine quantities, you can experiment at home. If you want oatmeal every morning, for example, find out just how much rolled oats are needed to make the breakfast you will likely eat in the woods. Just as a suggestion, take at least double the amount of sugar and sweets you would use at home, for your desire for them on the trail will be out of all proportion to what you want in the city.

All this takes time. But it will pay off in satisfaction, and it's fun.

The Most for the Least Trouble

Fat is, in calories, the most concentrated food. Butter, oleomargarine, and lard have double and triple the amount of calories that even such a quick-energy food as honey contains. If you plan to augment your meals with fish, the staples you carry should include a reasonable proportion of edible fats.

Other concentrated foods that have figured conspicuously in rations where space and weight have been stringently restricted include dried shelled nuts, peanut butter, chocolate, dried whole eggs, dried whole milk, and malted milk tablets. If you want a bulky starch, rice cooks up appetizingly with nearly everything.

You can, with weight and space at such an extreme premium, use a calorie chart as a basis for figuring how to go about packing the most nourishment with the least trouble. Briefly, you're burning up a certain amount of energy every second. Energy not supplied directly by a sufficiency of food is taken from the body's carbohydrates, fats, and proteins.

Even when you're sleeping relaxed in the most comfortable of eiderdowns, your system is consuming heat units (or calories) at the rate of approximately ten calories a day per pound of body weight. In other words, if you weigh 160 pounds, the least number of calories you'll use each day is 1,600. These basic requirements diminish but slightly, as a matter of fact, even when an individual is starving.

The more you move around and the more energy you expend in keeping warm, the more calories you use. Even lying in your sleeping bag on a stormy day and reading will increase your basic calorie needs about 25 per cent. The city man who gets very little exercise consumes on the average about 50 per cent above his minimum requirements. To maintain his weight, therefore, such a 160-pound individual requires about 2,400 calories daily.

It is reasonable, both from these scientific facts and from personal experience, to generalize that a healthy and fit man enjoying a robust outdoor life can require 25 calories of food a day per pound of body weight—and perhaps more, depending on the trail and on the climate. Cold weather, for example, compels the system to put out more and more heat to keep itself warm. The same 160-pound man hiking one of the great trails can very easily take in 4,000 calories a day, and more, and still trim down lean and hard.

Suitable Food Containers

Available inexpensively from a number of outdoor outfitters, small plastic bags are excellent for packing all home mixes and other dry foods suggested in this book. These bags can be readily sealed by a hot iron. If you may want to reuse them on the trail, close them instead with one of the adhesive cellulose tapes.

It's a good idea to repackage all dry foods whenever this can be done advantageously—in the case of something like cornflakes, breaking them down to the smallest possible bulk. Any special instructions should be cut out and enclosed.

Lightweight unbreakable plastic bottles and flasks in a wide variety of styles and shapes are on the market. You can get these to carry cooking oil and other inert liquids. The storing of whisky and liquors in polyethylene is safe for periods of up to two and three months.

Both regular and high-density polyethylene containers are suitable for vanilla extracts. However, they have not proved satisfactory with other extracts, because the aldehydes and esters in these cause a softening of the polyethylene. Such extracts, if you want to bother with any—perhaps for a feast of snowbank ice cream in the high mountains—are better left in their original glass containers, which may be wrapped in tape for safety.

Although high-density polyethylenes have been found suitable for use with spices, the essential oils present in significant quantities in black pepper, nutmeg, mace, etc. attack regular-density containers of this sort.

Lard, oleomargarine, butter, and the like travel well

in tightly closed aluminum or plastic containers. A handy way to carry a small amount of spread is by inserting it in the large open end of a tube similar to a toothpaste tube, obtainable at a supplier's or a drugstore, then sealing this by crimping.

The Need for Natural Sweets

You can buy one of several so-called sugar substitutes, one tiny pellet of which will sweeten a cup of coffee to the same degree as would a teaspoon of white sugar. Don't do it under ordinary circumstances unless for dietary reasons. The minute pills furnish the taste, certainly. But they add no fuel to the body.

The various natural sweets such as sugar are among our most readily assimilated energy foods. Granulated white sugar provides roundly 1,750 calories per pound. An equal amount of brown sugar contains 1,670 calories. The same amount of pure maple sugar has 1,580 calories. A pound of honey has 1,400 calories. Good jams average some 1,260 calories per pound, jellies slightly less. Some of the high-energy candy bars available from hiking outfitters pack in as many as 1,888 calories per pound. For comparison, one pound of fresh lean venison runs about 630 calories. In other words, this isn't the department in which mistakenly to try to save weight.

Dining on the Wild Foods

These days you can dine about as easily and well in the wilderness as in the city. Matter of fact, you're likely to find yourself eating considerably better. There may be the disadvantage of not being able to pick up many of the frozen specialities featured in modern markets. But this drawback is more than off-set by all the fresh foods that are at hand, free for the taking.

Whenever you learn how to recognize a reasonable number of these wild edibles, you're sort of like the old prospector who kneels on a lode of silver while he pans gold and platinum from a creek. Whatever your epicurean whim of the moment may be, you can satisfy it.

Fats for Camp Use

Oleomargarine, largely because it keeps so well, is recommended for general camp use. The camp shortening supply can be replenished by pouring in your surplus bacon grease, which is rich in calories and flavor. Tip the liquid grease into some handy container, such as a friction-top can, where it will harden and become easy to pack.

Jams and Marmalades

An outdoor trip is where you really appreciate jams and marmalades. Some hikers are bothered by the white crystals that often form in these foods. Looking like mold, such crystals tend to spread through the mixture once the first of them has appeared. Actually, they're the result of sugar combining with water in the preparation. Although they do nothing for texture and appearance, they are not at all harmful.

How to Pack Your Cheese

Cheese is one of the most versatile and delectable of camp foods. It may be relished in its natural state or added to everything from soups and salads to sauces, to make all sorts of delicious combinations. More than one day I've enjoyed it at breakfast with scrambled eggs, at lunch in a sandwich browned over the noonday tea fire, and at night with macaroni. Preferences vary. A sharp, aged Cheddar keeps well, as do Edam and Gouda. Provolone is probably the best choice in high temperatures.

If heat makes the cheese rubbery, a solution is to wrap it well and to revive it in a cool stream. If you're going to cache food beforehand to pick up periodically on the hike, sew one-week portions snugly in cheesecloth and immerse them in melted wax. You can harmlessly keep mold off cheese to a large extent by wiping the cheese with a clean cloth soaked in baking powder solution.

Spices and Flavorings

Everyone has his own ideas on these. Nearly everyone wants a little pepper. Small containers of powdered (not salt) onions, celery, and garlic pack a lot of possibilities. Paprika and powdered parsley combine taste and eye appeal. Then there are nutmeg, cinnamon, and their ilk. Like the rest, they cost only a few cents and occupy little room.

Among the flavorings that seem to taste particularly good in the woods are vanilla, banana, and the peppermint that really touches up chocolate. Then there are lemon and other pure fruit powders, crystals, etc. Suit yourself.

Convenient Trail Coffee

The way I like to make trail coffee is to put a rather coarse grind into fresh cold water, using two level tablespoons for every cup of water. Amounts can be varied, of course, for a stronger or weaker brew. Hang or set this over the fire. Watch it carefully. As soon as it boils up once, lift it to a warm sanctuary to take on body for five minutes. Then settle the grounds if you want with a couple of tablespoons of cold water and start pouring.

Unless you have decided preference to the contrary, though, powdered instant coffee is far preferable to the ground for general trail use—except perhaps for those first odiferous cups in the morning. It is more economical in weight and bulk, cheaper, better lasting, and quicker and easier to prepare. It can be made to individual order and without waste.

If you'd like to pocket several pleasant pickups before hitting the trail in the morning or before leaving it for a day's fishing, you can ready a number of these in a jiffy beforehand. For each, mix one teaspoon of your favorite instant coffee with an equal amount of sugar. Roll securely in foil. Dissolved pleasantly in the mouth, each will provide the same amount of stimulation and energy as would a similarly based cup of black coffee.

B'iling the Kittle for Tea

The northern woodsman, particularly the Canadian, must sip his steaming cup of tea at noon, even if he has nothing to eat. This is almost a religion up under the Aurora Borealis, and it's called "b'iling the kittle." Only a temporary fire is needed, a mere handful of dry wood that will flare up briefly and as quickly fall to ashes, a few specks of which invariably seem to swirl up to float unheeded in the dark brew. Get the water bubbling. Drop in a roughly measured teaspoon of tea for every cup of water, and set immediately from the heat in a safe place. Five minutes of steeping is sufficient.

Tea is something I've long preferred to carry in the usual form, if only for the pleasant rite of tossing a handful of palm-measured leaves into the bubbling kettle. There is powdered tea on the market, however, that mixes immediately with water and which tastes a lot closer to regular tea than any of the old powdered coffees used to taste like regularly brewed coffee. This tea can't reasonably be spoiled by improper making—unless some camp cook, by trying to make enough for everyone at once, somehow manages to boil it.

Fruit Juices and Soups

Fruit juices, available now in crystals and powders, are particular treats in the bush. Lemon, for example, is welcome with fresh rainbow trout.

Bouillon cubes and powders make hot drinks that taste good around a campfire. A lot of times you'll appreciate them more than you would either tea or coffee. They are also useful for flavoring broths, soups, gravies, and stews. Other worthwhile beverage concentrates include cocoa, malted milk, and chocolate.

Hot Chocolate and Cocoa

Hot chocolate and cocoa in particular have a way of easing those last few steps between fire and bed. As for chocolate bars, these are one of the best known and liked energy foods. It is a common thing on extended hikes to find a whitish appearance in such chocolate. This does not indicate spoilage, but is due to cocoa butter that has separated out. At a temperature no more than eighty-five degrees, the cocoa butter in ordinary chocolate melts and comes to the surface. It whitens upon hardening. Only the appearance of the chocolate is affected.

Snacks That Give You Energy

There's sound reason for snacking along the route, if that's what you like to do. Besides supplying quick energy, such snacking can prevent hunger from building up so intensely that you may lunch too heavily before you reach your next camp, thereby setting up a duel between the digestive and muscular functions of the system, leading to indigestion or sluggishness or both.

Something like raisins is particularly satisfying when you're walking along. So are some of the new freeze-dried fruits. Pemmican, little known and eaten these years, is ideal if you can come by any. Any manufactured products labeled "pemmican" that I have sampled during the last few years have been a far cry from real pemmican, actually roughly one-half rendered fat and one-half well-dried lean meat.

Wilson, however, puts out a 513-calorie, fully cooked meat bar which weighs only three ounces and is the equivalent of one pound of fat raw meat. This is available from the catalog-issuing outfitters in trail equipment, who also generally have a comprehensive selection of other tasty, high-energy foods especially designed for trail snacking.

Especially delicious and nutritious along the trail also are chunks of that heavy fruitcake that ordinarily seems a little too rich for city consumption.

11/All the Instant Foods

11

Improved Dehydrated Foods

Such words as pemmican, jerky, parched corn, buccan, and pinole are reminders that dehydrated foods were important along the trails of this country even during flintlock days. The basic formula has not changed. It is to remove as much moisture from the edible portion of the particular food as may be practicable. Drying by sun and wind often extracted no more than three-fourths of this water. Modern processes sometimes leave less than one per cent.

Old-time hikers did not have much affection for most of the commercially dried foods, with the exception of a few such as peas, beans, and the fruits. There has been a tremendous improvement in dehydrated foods since the time of the Korean crisis. Most of the new dessicated foods are simple and speedy to prepare temptingly, usually requiring only water, heat, and occasionally a whit of discriminating seasoning. Few now require lengthy presoaking. Most take no more than ten to twenty or so minutes to prepare.

Dried apples and apricots have long been camp favorites, saving considerable weight and bulk as they do, while doing away with the worries of spoil-

age and freezing. Pears and peaches have their advocates, and there is always the prune. Such items as
raisins, currants, figs, and dates round out many a list.

Prepared before they are processed and packaged,
low-moisture fruits go into the pack in practical, convenient form, ready for use. They do not have to be
washed, rinsed, peeled, cored, or sliced, but can be
used just as they come from the package, often as
quick snacks along the route. There is no waste, no
disposal of waste material, to worry about. Even the
parts of cores that used to embellish dried apples
are gone.

Dehydration by Freeze-Drying

That's not all. One pound of the new applesauce
freeze-dried mix—taking the place of ten pounds of
fresh whole apples—replaces two and three-fourths
pounds of the old-style evaporated apples. A pound
of the new apricot slices, besides replacing some six
and two-thirds pounds of canned wet apricots, comes
in place of two and one-half pounds of old evaporated apricots with all their familiar virtues. It's the
same with the new peach slices, whole pitted prunes,
and fruit mix. Ease of preparation and delicious natural flavor as well have been stepped up. As a matter
of fact, color, flavor, and nutritive qualities are virtually equal to the fresh, and to the pick of the fresh at
that.

The way freeze-drying works is similar to how
clothes dry in freezing weather. Many a subzero day
my wife has filled the line outside our far-northern
log cabin with wash which immediately froze stiff.

Although the cold snap continued, the clothes still dried, because of water's unique property of being able to change from a solid to a vapor without melting.

Carefully trimmed and readied foods, some of them already cooked, are frozen. They are then placed in a vacuum chamber, in minutely controlled heat, where their moisture is gently vaporized away. That is, the ice crystals disperse without ever melting to a liquid, in a phenomenon we used to know in physics as sublimation. Generally, some 98 per cent of the original moisture in the foodstuffs is floated away in this fashion.

The food at this stage, even with nearly all the water removed, looks amazingly like the original, particularly in size and shape. As might be anticipated, however, its surface greatly resembles that of a cellulose sponge. It is about as thirsty. So that it will be prevented from drinking the moisture in the air, the food is hurried into airtight plastic, foil, and other containers. Thus protected, it can be stored for months without refrigeration and without deterioration, until reconstituted in camp by the addition of a specified amount of liquid obtained on the spot. There is another boon. Foods packed in this manner have no odors to attract hungry animals.

Delicious New Dried Meats

One of the greatest breakthroughs afforded by freeze-drying—called the greatest innovation in the food field since the invention of the tin can—is in the preservation of meat. You can now hike a couple of weeks away from the nearest supply point and each night, farther and farther back of beyond, sit down to tender juicy beefsteaks.

Porkchops, hamburgers, sliced beef, and other such meats are available, too. For concentrated lunching en route, Wilson is marketing a pressed beef and pork bar that's ready to eat. It requires no refrigeration nor cooking, although it can be turned into delicious soup. Its three ounces provide over 500 calories. Wilson also has a bacon bar of similar weight, made of pressed prefried bacon that can be tastily crumbled in eggs, over potatoes, or into soup; or it can be carried in a handy pocket for munching along the trail.

The first time you ever do it in the wilderness, it's quite an event when you open one of, say, Armour's Star Lite foil packets and look in at the light, porous steaks that tip the scales at about one-fourth of their original weight. You mix a small package of accompanying seasoning with cold water and pour it into the handy packet, which thus does away with need for an extra dish—a great boon in trail cookery.

As the meat's cells refill with fluid, the hemoglobin which was still present in the dried steak reunites with water to form fresh blood that starts to turn the water pink. In fifteen minutes the steaks, now full-bodied and red, are ready for the fry pan. After a couple or so minutes of cooking on each side, they're tender and startlingly delicious.

Although it's not necessary, I like to spread margarine liberally on both sides of such reconstituted meat before consigning it to the heat, both for flavor and to help prevent the added moisture from boiling away. In any event, plenty of such fat will add to the flavor, as in the processing all the natural fat that can be removed is trimmed away. So is all bone and waste. What's left is all meat, which was the choicest available to begin with.

New Freeze-Dried Vegetables

Freeze-drying does not always conserve much in the way of bulk. But some of its greatest reductions in bulk are in connection with vegetables (whose reconstituted natural flavor and color are now a far cry from what you used to get in the dehydrated vegetables that were on the market).

It is now possible to pack enough carrots into a two-ounce package to furnish sixteen servings when water is added. Vegetables with higher water contents furnish even more dramatic savings. Cabbage, to give one example, is some nine-tenths water, setting the stage for fitting eighty pounds of what was fresh cabbage into a can about the size of a flat tin of tuna, weighing two and one-half pounds.

Disadvantages of Freeze-Dried Foods

As with most new products, there are still some disadvantages to freeze-dried foods that are receiving concentrated attention. Even with the savings afforded by lower transportation costs and far fewer storage problems, freeze-dried foods remain generally expensive for campers. Because many of the products, including the meats, retain much of their original size and are liable to crush or chip, the constantly improving packaging is still often bulky.

Flavors, although greatly superior to those of other

dried foods, are still not always equal to that of the fresh product—although that may sometimes mean you'll like it better. Fresh turnips are not one of my favorite vegetables, for example, but to my taste the dried varieties are just about tops. For my particular palate, both Armour's Chili with Beans and the Shrimp Creole are the equal of any I've eaten in Mexico or Louisiana.

Some processors tend toward complicated multi-course repasts, whereas the hiker is most interested in a meal he can prepare with one pot and one frypan.

But when you're back in the mountains, sitting down to a savory feast fit for the home table, and hungry enough to enjoy it, the above shortcomings seem meager indeed. This is especially true because in these days you can easily backpack as much food as, in the old days, would have bent the spine of a good-sized packhorse.

Eat It If You Enjoy It

With new foods forthcoming each year since commercial freeze-dried items were introduced to this country's market in about 1959, over a hundred different products are now available at this writing. I have tried many of these. Almost all are faithfully comparable to the fresh products, and I very much like nearly all. Naturally a few I don't care for, just as I prefer to pass up their fresh equivalents.

The point is that it is best in general for a hiker to eat on the trail approximately the way he does in day-by-day living. This is to avoid the unpleasantness of physiological conversion. The psychological values of foods are of special importance during the usual short hikes. It's true enough that there is no physical necessity for steaks, vegetables, and fruits if instead, for example, you eat genuine pemmican and vitamin pills exclusively. But if the craving for the former is not satisfied, morale takes a beating. And you're out for pleasure.

In other words, try the dehydrated products first. It is most satisfactory to do this food by food; but sampling two or three items from any one company will, in practice, pretty well establish your liking for the whole line. Do this testing before you leave home. Tastes differ. A major error is to load up with dehydrated meals for the entire trip, especially some of those dried by older methods, without everyone's doing considerable sampling beforehand. Ordinarily you'll be heading out for fun and relaxation, and the enjoyment of your meals is going to be a determining factor.

With well over a dozen U. S. processors now in operation, there is plenty of freeze-dried food to choose from. In general, any food that freezes well will freeze-dry. Foods high in fat or sugars are difficult to freeze-dry, because they freeze poorly. Foods such as melons and cucumbers freeze, but because of their loose physical structure they will not easily rehydrate back to their original form. In other words, the possibilities, with a few exceptions, are virtually unlimited.

It is possible to pick up many dehydrated items at even small grocery stores. Instant potatoes are an example. Numerous soup powders, certainly one of freeze-drying's most successful offshoots, are widely available. Macaroni, noodles, spaghetti, and their ilk are already pretty well dehydrated, but now the hiker can buy different dry sauce mixes with which to season and flavor them. From among the instantly mixed puddings needing only water, the hiker may select lemon, butterscotch, orange, coconut, banana, vanilla, maple, pumpkin, and even tangerine.

Brands Worth Considering

I've just had the pleasure of retesting under trail conditions the pre-assembled meals and other dehydrated foods designed for hiking by Chuck Wagon Foods, Micro Drive, Woburn, Massachusetts 01801. Both Vena and I find them sustaining and enjoyable, as well as light, compact, and efficiently packed. Sidney L. Morrison is the president of this company, and F. Harmon Saville is plant manager. Both are alert to knapsack needs.

Another expert in this field with whom you might profitably get in touch is William B. White, Stow-A-Way Products, Cohasset, Massachusetts 02025, who has exclusively outfitted a commanding array of scientific survey groups with field and emergency rations. I've also retested his backpacking foods and find them better than ever.

Varieties of Dehydrated Milk

As far as nutrition goes, both powdered milk and eggs compare favorably with the fresh products. Which taste you prefer is mostly a matter of what you're accustomed to. In other words, nothing is the matter with either one, and you can become satisfied with each, as I can personally testify from long use in the wilderness.

Depending on the product, one pound of whole milk powder makes one gallon of liquid whole milk. This powder is sometimes a little difficult to mix with water, but there are several ways to get around this. When you open the container, stir the powder and lightly take up the amount you want, without packing it down in any way. Even measures are best obtained by leveling off the top of the cup or spoon with the straight edge of a knife. Place the powder on top of the water with which it is to mix. Then stir with a spoon until smooth. The mixing can be speeded somewhat by having the water slightly warm. You can also shake the water and powder together in a tightly closed jar which will subsequently serve as a pitcher.

Better spray dryers have improved the quality of dehydrated milk. The quick-hydrating quality of newer skim milk powders, however, is the result of a second drying step which gives the particles a porous, spongelike fluffiness that required thirty years of research to achieve.

Dried skimmed milk has all the nourishment of fresh skimmed milk. It has the calcium, phosphorous, iron and other minerals, the B vitamins, natural sugar, and the protein that make liquid skimmed milk such an important food.

Powdered whole milk has all these, plus the fat and Vitamin A found in the cream of whole milk. Adding two teaspoons of margarine or butter to a cup of reconstituted skimmed milk will make this equal in food value to a cup of whole milk. And it is a lot easier to mix.

You can even use dried skimmed milk to make a whipped topping for wild berries. Mix one-half cup of the milk powder with one-half cup of preferably icy water. Beat for three or four minutes until soft peaks form. Then add two tablespoons of reconstituted lemon juice and beat about the same length of time until it is stiff. Fold in one-quarter cup sugar. About three cups of topping will result. Serve on raspberries, strawberries, or what you will while you're still ahead.

Containers holding any of the dry milk products should be kept tightly closed, as the powder attracts moisture and becomes lumpy if long exposed to the air. It also picks up odors unless care is taken.

Powdered milk mixed dry with flour makes a valuable addition to biscuits and bannock. Mornings when you're in a hurry to get on the trail, milk powder can be mixed directly with cereals such as oatmeal and the breakfast food then cooked as indicated on the package.

Powdered and Freeze-Dried Eggs

An egg is 11 per cent waste. All of 74 per cent of the remaining yolk and white is water. Yet a dried whole egg has virtually the same food value, includes no waste whatsoever, and is only some 5 per cent water.

More efficient processing equipment and methods have greatly improved the quality of all dried eggs. Varying somewhat with brands, a pound of dessicated eggs is the equivalent of some five dozen fresh eggs. One level tablespoon of the yellow solid beaten until smoothly blended with two tablespoons of water, again depending on the individual product, equals one hen's egg.

The flavor of egg powder cooked by itself is not like that of fresh eggs. Most of us in the United States are accustomed to the latter.

In any event, scrambled eggs prepared from the powder come to taste mighty good in the farther places. If you haven't prepared these before, dissolve powdered eggs and milk in lukewarm water to make the proportions of these fresh products you ordinarily use. Add salt, pepper, and any other seasoning, together with a chunk of margarine or bacon grease. A little flour may be stirred in for thickening. Scrambling all this with ham or bacon gives the dish added flavor. With the new crystalline freeze-dried eggs, you don't even have to go to this much trouble.

12/The Trail Cook

12

Baking Bannock Outdoors

While the body is making the change from a city diet comparatively high in bulk to relatively concentrated trail food, it is a good idea to get up from meals feeling not quite satisfied. Trying to fill up with concentrated foods can lead to sluggishness and digestive troubles. On the other hand, it's not much fun to be hungry all the time, either actually or psychologically. A practical and satisfying way to fill up those empty places is with the easily made frypan bread known as "bannock."

About the only cooking odors that even approach the aroma of bannock-baking outdoors are the sizzling smell of good grilled bacon, coffee bubbling in the heat of a campfire, and fat steak sputtering over hard wood coals.

This is just as well; because unless you replenish it frequently, bakery bread soon becomes moldy, stale, and thoroughly unappetizing in the out-of-doors. And its airy softness is bulky and unsubstantial when it comes to packing. All these shortcomings are especially apparent when you consider that even the rankest greenhorn can break himself off a hot chunk of this steaming frypan bread after a few minutes of practically foolproof effort.

The basic recipe for one hungry hiker follows. If you want more, just increase these ingredients proportionally: one cup of flour, one teaspoon of baking powder, and one-fourth teaspoon of salt.

Mix these dry if you're starting from scratch, taking all the time you need to do this thoroughly. Have the hands floured and everything ready to go before you add liquid. Make sure the frying pan is warm and greased.

Working quickly from now on, stir in enough cold water to make a firm dough. Shape this, with as little handling as possible, into a cake about an inch thick. If you like crust, leave a doughnut-like hole in the middle. Dust the loaf lightly with flour so it will handle more easily.

Lay the bannock in the warm frying pan. Hold it over the heat until a bottom crust forms, rotating the pan a little so the loaf will shift and not become stuck.

Once the dough has hardened enough to hold together, you can turn the bannock. This, if you've practiced a bit and have the confidence to flip strongly enough, can easily be accomplished with a slight swing of the arm and snap of the wrist. Or you can use one of the plates from your cooking outfit, sliding the bannock onto this and then reversing the frypan over the plate and turning both together.

With a campfire, however, it is often easier at this stage just to prop the frypan at a steep angle so that the bannock will get direct heat on top. When crust has formed all around, you may if you wish turn the bannock over and around a few times while it is baking to an appetizing golden brown.

When is the bannock done? After you've been cooking them awhile, you will be able to tap one and gauge this by the hollowness of the sound. Meanwhile test by shoving in a clean straw or sliver. If any dough adheres, the loaf needs more heat. Cooking can be accomplished in about fifteen minutes. If you have other duties around camp, twice that time a bit farther from the heat will allow the bannock to cook more evenly.

Other Ways of Cooking It

Instead of slanting the pan in front of the fire to cook the top side only, you can often bake it throughout at this second stage. This can be accomplished by the use of an existing boulder or some other such reflecting surface, perhaps several large stones laid up beside the campfire for this purpose. When the reflecting area is hot, lean the pan with its back to this and its face to the direct heat.

You can also scoop a small pit in front of the campfire, rake a few red-hot coals into it, and set the frypan on these so the bannock will be cooked both by the embers below and the blazing forelog of the fire above. For best results, this forelog should be a wellburning one that's lying several inches off the ground at this point and blazing upwards with a generally vertical flame.

Suppose you're short on utensils and long on appetites. As soon as each loaf is crusty enough to hold its shape, slide it out of the pan and lean it on the ground near enough to the campfire to finish cooking. Immediately start another.

Bannock never tastes better than when devoured

piping hot around a campfire. It should then be broken apart, never cut. A cold bannock sliced in half, however, and made into a man-sized sandwich with plenty of meat or other filler in between is the best lunch ever.

Things to Know About Baking Powder

When liquid is added to baking powder, gas is released. This is the same harmless carbon dioxide that gives such beverages as ginger ale their bubbliness. Its function in breadstuffs is to raise the dough. Without some such effervescence you'd wind up with a chunk of hardtack (the way to make hardtack, incidentally).

It follows that you want to prevent as much as possible of this gas from wastefully escaping. Aside from speed, you can conserve it in several ways. Cold fluid, as might be expected, releases the carbon dioxide more slowly than hot. It is also better to do so much of the necessary mixing as possible with a cold spoon or peeled stick rather than with the warm hands.

Why not just put in more baking powder? The answer is that food tastes better and digests more easily with a minimum of this acid-alkali combination. Some trail cooks do tend to take out insurance by using more than the teaspoon of baking powder that's generally sufficient for each cup of flour.

It's true that strengths of this leavening agent vary. Furthermore, all baking powder tends to become weaker with age, particularly if the container has not been kept tightly closed and in a dry and preferably cool place. It's sound practice to stir baking powder a bit before measuring, partly to break up any lumps but mainly to assure a more uniform mixture of ingredients. The outer layer is apt to lose some of its leavening power because of contact with the air.

Directions on the particular can if the contents are fresh, and experimentation if they are not, will provide a functional yardstick if you've any doubts. Double-action baking powder, the so-called combination type which releases part of its gas when heated, packs more power than either the tartrate or the calcium phosphate varieties. The recipes in this book are geared to it.

The ideal, insofar as flavor and digestion are concerned, is to use the smallest amount of baking powder that will raise the breadstuff enough for your liking.

What to Mix the Dough In

The easiest and most economical way of mixing dough is to carry a small sheet of thin plastic. Bark may also be used occasionally, but at best it's a nuisance. Wax paper or foil add too much weight.

Prospectors, trappers, and other professional outdoorsmen still widely continue the practice of mixing bannock right in the flour sacks themselves. Just make a little hollow in the flour. Drop the salt and baking powder into this. Then, stirring with the fingers of one hand, add the water gradually until the resulting dough has picked up all the flour it needs. Press and pat into shape. Cook.

Variations in the Recipe

Variations on the basic bannock recipe are innumerable. Including a tablespoon of sugar with every cup of flour will make for a more pronounced taste and crisper crust. Powdered eggs, the equivalent of one-half to one egg for every cup of flour, will add thickness and richness. The addition of powdered milk will improve both the flavor and the characteristic golden-brownness.

Adding a shortening, usually from one to three tablespoons per cup of flour, will increase tenderness. This is especially desirable when skiing enthusiasts take over some of these hiking trails, as in Vermont. Then even larger proportions of fat are sometimes necessary to keep the breadstuff from freezing hard on frost routes. Solids like butter, margarine, lard, and bacon drippings that keep accumulating are most effective when either creamed with the sugar or thoroughly mixed with the flour.

Such fruits as raisins, currants, and the berries—such as blueberries—that you pick along the way make bannock tastier, although their inclusion calls for the use of a bit more baking powder. Combine these fruits with the dry ingredients to avoid any overmixing. Spices, particularly nutmeg and cinnamon, are unusually zestful when their odors mingle with the keenness of pine trees and wood smoke.

Homemade Dry Bannock Mix . . .

You can make your own dehydrated biscuit and bannock mix. These fresh foods are simple things to cook on the trail. Then the handiest method is to mix the dry ingredients before leaving the base of supplies. In fact, you can make a number of such batches at home before the hiking vacation, sealing each in a small plastic bag. This mix has multiple short-notice uses.

The following basic mix, given here in generous one-hiker proportions, will stay fresh for six weeks or more on the trail if kept sealed, dry, and reasonably cool:

1 cup all-purpose flour
1 teaspoon double-action baking powder
¼ teaspoon salt
3 tablespoons oleomargarine

If this mix is being readied at home, sift the flour before measuring it. Then sift together the flour, baking powder, and salt. Cut in the margarine with two dull knives, with an electric mixer at low speed, or with a pastry blender, until the mixture resembles coarse meal. For increased food value in camp, add two tablespoons of powdered skimmed milk for every cup of flour.

Place in plastic bags. Seal with a hot iron or with one of the plastic tapes. A large quantity can be made at once and divided into smaller portions. Before using, it is a good idea to stir the mixture lightly.

If compounding this mix in camp, do it with the ingredients at hand and in the simplest way possible. Any solid shortening may be utilized if the mix is to be used within a short time. Such mix may be folded in wax paper for carrying.

For Hot Bread Along the Trail

This is handy when you're momentarily short of cooking utensils. When the fire is going and everything else is ready, quickly add enough water to the basic mix to make a firm dough. Shape into a long, thin roll no wider than an inch thick. Wind this ribbon on a preheated green hardwood stick the diameter of a rake handle, so trimmed that several projecting stubs of branches will keep the dough in place. A particularly sweet wood for the job is birch.

Hold the bannock in the heat, occasionally turning it, for a couple of minutes. Once a crust has been formed, the stick may be leaned between the fringes of the fire and some reflecting surface such as a log or rock for the fifteen minutes or so required to form a tasty brown spiral. Or you can just shove a sharpened end of the stick into the ground beside the fire and turn this holder now and then while readying the remainder of the meal.

For Regular Frypan Bread

When ready to go, add to the mix about one-third cup of cold water for an easily handled dough. Cook like regular bannock.

For Oven Drop Biscuits

When you hit a shelter with an oven, mix with a little less than half a cup of water to make a soft dough. Drop by the spoonful on top of a hot greased metal surface and bake in a very hot oven for ten to fifteen minutes.

For Baked Fruit Cobblers

Proceed as with the above biscuits, but drop each daub of dough on top of a frying section of apple, apricot, or other cooked dry fruit.

For Shortcakes in Berry Season

Add one tablespoon of sugar to make half a dozen medium-sized shortcakes, which will assure a pleasant change of diet in berry season. Mix with one-third cup of cold water to form an easily handled dough. Flatten this to one-quarter inch and either cut squares with a knife or punch out ovals with something like a can top. Cook like bannock. Then add margarine to the tops of half of the biscuits, and cover each of these with one of the remaining pieces. Serve hot with fruit.

For Flapjacks in Camp

Add half a cup of milk, with which the equivalent of one egg has been mixed, to the homemade dry mix. Stir only enough to moisten the flour. If the flapjack batter is still a bit too thick to pour easily, thin it with just enough milk. Flour, on the other hand, will provide stiffening. If the batter is on the thin side, the flippers will be more tender.

Once the frypan is hot, grease it sparingly with bacon drippings. Do not let the metal reach smoking temperatures. Turn each flapjack only once, when the hotcake starts showing little bubbles. The second side takes about half as long to cook. Serve steaming hot with margarine and sugar, with fruit, or with what you will.

For Delicious Hot Dumplings

Nothing sets off a hearty outdoor stew like steaming hot dumplings. These are a cinch to make, and they have the additional advantages of needing neither separate cooking nor extra washing. The following recipe should satisfy two ravenous hikers.

About a dozen minutes before mealtime, take the contents of two packets of mix. Make a bowl-like hollow in the center. Have everything ready to roll —for these dumplings should be cooked only eight to ten minutes, and then the meal should be served immediately. Have the broth simmering above enough meat and vegetables so that the dumplings will not sink beneath the surface.

Now pour one cup of reconstituted milk into the well in the middle of the dry ingredients. Mix quickly and gently with a folding, rather than a stirring or whipping, motion. Moisten a large spoon in the broth. Use it to place large spoonfuls, apart from one another, on top of the stew. Cover tightly. After several minutes you may, if you want, turn each dumpling carefully and speedily. Recover immediately and continue simmering until light and fluffy.

Then serve without delay. If any dumplings remain for second helpings, place them in a separate hot dish so that they won't become soggy.

The Best Way to Cook Bacon

The main troubles that trail cooks experience with bacon arise from their submitting it too soon to too much heat. Not only is the bacon thus burned and toughened, but very often the frypan becomes a mass of leaping flames. Aside from resulting offenses to taste and digestion, this is wasteful. The nearly 3,000 calories per pound that fat side bacon contains lie largely in its grease, any excess of which should be saved, particularly when you're backpacking.

We'll do better to start the bacon in a cold frying pan and fry it slowly over a very few coals raked to one side of the blaze. Move and turn the bacon from time to time. If you like it crisp, keep pouring off the grease. Don't waste any of this though; it has numerous camp uses.

Slabs of bacon have a tendency to mold. This mold can be wiped off with a clean cloth moistened in a solution of baking soda and water or, if you have any, in vinegar.

Cooking Dried Beans and Peas

The various dried beans and their cousins the dried peas and lentils are favorite old-time dehydrated foods. All provide hearty nourishment because of their carbohydrates, which the body transforms in energy. They contain some B vitamins. Besides such minerals as iron and calcium, they furnish protein which the body needs for building and repairing its organs and tissues. They are both inexpensive and fairly easy to prepare.

Although split peas and lentils can be cooked without soaking, the ordinary beans may be soaked overnight. Preferably, however, they can be started cooking by first bringing the water to a boil for two minutes. After they have then been soaked an hour, they will be ready to cook. The brief precooking, besides saving time, will guard against any souring if they are to be prepared in warm weather. Cooking should be done in the same water, both to preserve flavor and to conserve minerals and vitamins. Here is the whole story.

Start with one cup of	Soak in water	Add one teaspoon salt; boil gently	Will yield at least
black beans	3 cups	about 2 hours	2 cups
blackeye beans	2½ cups	½ hour	2½ cups
cranberry beans	3 cups	about 2 hours	2 cups
great northern beans	2½ cups	1 to 1½ hours	2½ cups
kidney beans	3 cups	about 2 hours	2½ cups
lentils	2½ cups	½ hour	2½ cups
lima beans, large	2½ cups	1 hour	2½ cups
lima beans, small	2½ cups	about 45 minutes	2 cups
navy (pea) beans	3 cups	about 2½ hours	2½ cups
peas, split	best made into soup as they break up easily during cooking		
peas, whole	2½ cups	1 hour	2½ cups
pinto beans	3 cups	about 2 hours	2½ cups

But if you are bean-hungry and don't want to waste even that much time over the fire, you can heat up a meal of processed and cleaned quick-cooking beans in a few minutes. Directions are given on the packages.

Like the old German Erbswurst, pea and bean powders now available also make excellent and filling soups with a minimum of time and trouble. Stir such concentrates into hot water and bring everything to a simmer, making the soup as thick or thin as you like.

Making Ice Cream with Snow

Ice cream is one of the quickest and easiest of all desserts to make outdoors, especially after a fresh snow. Best for the purpose are dry flakes. You can also use the granular interior of the perpetual snowbanks found in the higher mountains, although the result will be more a coarse sherbet.

Just make two cups of reconstituted dry milk in a large pan. Add two tablespoons of sugar, one-eighth teaspoon of salt, and some flavoring. Vanilla or one of the other extracts will do. So will cocoa, powdered coffee, and the like. For mocha, balance two teaspoons of powdered instant coffee with half a teaspoon of chocolate—enough, incidentally, for a quart of ice cream.

Then quickly stir in fresh snow to taste. More sweetening and flavoring may be added at the end if you want. It is safest to go light on these initially. Otherwise you'll have to repair any mistake with more milk and snow—not that this isn't a good excuse.

Three varieties that come out especially well, if you happen to like them to begin with, are the universally favored vanilla, rich dark chocolate (with perhaps overtones of peppermint extract), and banana ice cream made with that particular extract.

Preparing Your Breakfast Cereal

Prepare according to the instructions on the package. In nearly every case, repack. If the cereal is unnecessarily bulky, reduce in size as much as possible.

A favorite trail cereal of a lot of us is oatmeal. The quickly cooking variety saves time. What I do is ready it the night before by adding one-half cup of oatmeal and one-half teaspnoon of salt to two cups of cold water. A quarter cup of raisins, more or less, plump out overnight to add flavor.

The next morning I hunch far enough out of the sleeping bag to get the fire going, put on the covered pan, and let the contents come to a boil before setting it to one side for a few minutes. Then I add a liberal spoonful of margarine and begin satisfying the inner man.

This, like a lot of things that would be just ordinary experiences elsewhere, is a real luxury on a cold, beautiful morning when you're way out in the woods somewhere.

Index

Index